Praise for *A Tender Struggle*
(previously published as *My Accidental Jihad*)

"Touchingly comic . . . What elevates it to a great read is the author's ability to fully evoke her emotional and sensory memories . . . Bremer's story isn't so much about cultural clashes as it is about something deeper; it's one woman's attempt to really understand—and be understood by—the person she loves. And at the root of it, isn't that what all of us hope for?"　　—*Elle*

"In elegant prose, Bremer recounts her unlikely love story and explores her discomfort with her husband's cultural and spiritual norms . . . A thought-provoking exploration of the deep foreignness of marriage, and a moving portrait of love, tolerance and family."　　—*Shelf Awareness for Readers*

"Utterly absorbing . . . A beautiful book."
　　　　　　　　　　　　—Cheryl Strayed, author of *Wild*

"This is a marriage with more than the usual differences . . . It's in Libya that Bremer has a key insight about bicultural marriages: Not all differences are cultural; Ismail may be 'maddening on *both* sides of the world' . . . A very good story."
　　　　　　　　　　　　—*The New York Times*

"A bold piece of writing (and thinking) by an incredibly brave woman."　　—Elizabeth Gilbert, author of *Eat, Pray, Love*

"Candid and rich."   —*Good Housekeeping*

"A beautiful account of [Krista's] jihad, or struggle, to find peace within herself and within her marriage." —*The Kansas City Star*

"Lucid, heartfelt and profoundly humane, *My Accidental Jihad* navigates the boundaries of religion and politics to arrive at the universal experience of love."
                        —G. Willow Wilson, author of *Alif the Unseen*

"A story about love, marriage, compromise, parenthood and the difference between the life one imagined and reality . . . Readers will be captivated by the book's love story while empathizing with Ms. Bremer throughout her journey. This is a memoir worth reading."   —*Pittsburgh Post-Gazette*

"Told with rare honesty, *My Accidental Jihad* is the story of Krista Bremer's lifelong quest for insight and understanding, a search that leads her out of the Pacific surf to journalism school in North Carolina and through the complex challenges and unexpected joys of a cross-cultural marriage and family. This book is a powerfully personal account of the courage and hard work necessary to open one's heart and keep it that way."
                        —Maggie Shipstead, author of *Seating Arrangements*

"A book about becoming more introspective—about how *any* successful and lasting marriage involves as much self-reckoning as compromise."   —*Los Angeles Review of Books*

"Readers of memoir will welcome this love story about patience and kindness and learning the importance of putting culture first." —*Library Journal*

"A moving, lyrical memoir about how an American essayist fell in love with a Libyan-born Muslim man and learned to embrace the life she made with him . . . A sweet and rewarding journey of a book." —*Kirkus Reviews*

"One of the most captivating and moving memoirs I've read in years. The story Krista Bremer tells—one of radical foreignness between a married couple—could be a metaphor for all committed relationships."
—Haven Kimmel, author of *A Girl Named Zippy*

"[An] insightful memoir . . . Bremer's [book] is much more than a love story. It is an invitation for its readers to examine their own selves." —*The Roanoke Times*

"Unrelenting candor and gorgeous prose . . . The brilliance of this book is that the author never lets herself or her husband off the hook. Instead, she presents an honest—and at times painful—portrayal of a beautiful union." —*BookPage*

"Bremer's particular story strikingly highlights the (usually more mundane) cultural clashes and compromises inherent to every marriage or long-term relationship."
—*Publishers Weekly*

A Story
Tender of a
Struggle Marriage

KRISTA BREMER

ALGONQUIN BOOKS OF CHAPEL HILL 2015

Published by
Algonquin Books of Chapel Hill
Post Office Box 2225
Chapel Hill, North Carolina 27515-2225

a division of
Workman Publishing
225 Varick Street
New York, New York 10014

First paperback edition, Algonquin Books of Chapel Hill, March 2015.
Originally published in hardcover as *My Accidental Jihad*
by Algonquin Books of Chapel Hill, April 2014.
Printed in the United States of America.
Published simultaneously in Canada by Thomas Allen & Son Limited.
Design by Anne Winslow.

The Library of Congress has cataloged
the hardcover edition of this book as follows:
Bremer, Krista.
My accidental jihad : a love story /
Krista Bremer.—First edition.
pages cm
ISBN 978-1-61620-068-8 (HC)
1. Bremer, Krista.   2. Interethnic marriage.
3. North Carolina—Biography.   I. Title.
CT275.B6435A3 2014
975.6'044092—dc23
[B]   2013043143

ISBN 978-1-61620-449-5 (PB)

10 9 8 7 6 5 4 3 2 1
First Paperback Edition

For my children,
Aliya Rose and Khalil Zade

The lion who breaks the enemy's ranks
is a minor hero compared to the lion
who overcomes himself.

—MEWLANA JALALUDDIN RUMI

CONTENTS

Part III | *Homecoming*

I | *Homeland Insecurity*

1 | *Choices*

Back in 1994, after I stood up on a surfboard for the first time, I thought I might just have discovered my purpose in life. Nothing I'd ever done compared to the exhilaration of gliding across the face of a wave. I moved into a tiny beach apartment with a hairdresser and a full-time bodybuilder. Craning my head out my bedroom window, I could see a shimmering thread of the Pacific Ocean in the distance. This felt like a major accomplishment.

But I urgently needed a steady income, so I took a position as an assistant at a Planned Parenthood clinic. The job paid enough to cover my rent and was close enough to my apartment that I could walk to work. It was also in keeping with my feminist ideals. In my undergraduate women's studies classes, I'd found my tribe among classmates who debated passionately, laughed loudly, and dressed comfortably. In our discussions we sat in a circle on the floor, our unshaven legs tucked beneath us. We had heated discussions about gender constructs, institutionalized sexism, and whether a woman should feel self-conscious wearing a tampon at a nude beach. I had tossed off the artifacts of high school—curling irons, berry-flavored pink lip gloss, paralyzing self-consciousness—and discovered that it was acceptable, even desirable, to have a strong body and a critical mind. In my new job I looked forward to playing a role in empowering women.

In the mornings before work, I'd maneuver my heavy long board out of the apartment and walk down to the beach in the crisp dawn air, zipping up my wetsuit at the shoreline and then jogging into the surf. When my feet first hit the water, I'd recoil both from the cold that numbed my ankles and from the thought of being pulled under the gray waves. As much as I loved surfing, I was terrified of the ocean. Every morning I fought the impulse to turn back and stay on the sand, where it was warm and dry. Big waves sometimes appeared out of nowhere, tossing my heavy board as if it were a toothpick and pinning me against the ocean floor. The first time this had happened, I'd panicked, clawing desperately at the water while I spun like a sock in the laundry. It's impossible to know which way is up while you're being tossed by a wave, and I quickly learned that the more I struggled, the faster I depleted my oxygen supply. If I relaxed, however, my natural buoyancy would eventually float me back to the surface.

I'd get out of the water at 7:30 A.M., leaving just enough time to hurry back to my apartment; pull my dripping, matted hair into a ponytail; rinse the thin white crust of salt from my face; and make it to the clinic by eight. The job was perfect for me, a literature major with a voracious appetite for people's stories. Interviewing a client in my tiny office, our knees nearly touching, I felt like a music fanatic who'd landed a job at a record store.

Across from me usually sat a young woman around my age; many times I'd recognize her from the beach or campus. A recent graduate myself, I'd affect my best professional tone and sail through a list of questions about her medical history. I'd always pause awkwardly before asking "At what age did you first engage in sexual intercourse?" and "How many sexual partners have you had in the past year?" I'd save those two questions for last and note the answers with a brisk nod and a click of my pen, secretly comparing the woman's experiences to my own. But before asking those questions, I'd try to guess if the woman across from me had a more adventurous sex life than I did and whether she had lost her virginity at a younger age than I had. I usually guessed wrong. The middle-aged former prostitute with the bleached-blonde hair and leathery tan, who lingered in my office and wondered aloud how she would explain the twelve-year gap in her résumé to potential employers, had been with very few partners in the previous year. The young woman who showed up at the clinic wearing nylons in the middle of summer and looking as if she were there for a job interview had lost her virginity at an age when I was still having slumber parties.

In addition to taking medical histories, I administered hormone injections for birth control, described the benefits of the IUD, and once explained "the three bases" to a nervous boy who called the clinic after school and asked questions in a high-pitched voice. But the most dramatic part of the job was administering pregnancy tests. I could tell from a patient's eyes as she handed me her urine sample how she felt about possibly being pregnant. While she sat in the waiting room, I stood in the tiny laboratory, waiting to see whether the thin pink line on the dipstick would appear—first faint, then staining the white tip darker and darker, marking a permanent boundary between before and after.

I'd call the woman back into my office, maneuvering the folding door shut to provide an illusion of privacy. Most clients I saw did not want to be pregnant. When I confirmed their pregnancies, they sighed heavily and held their faces in their hands. I learned to sit in that confined space with a crying stranger, to hand her a tissue without saying anything.

With their copious tears and unpredictable reactions, these women made me anxious, and I was grateful for the color-coded information sheets I could hand them: purple for adoption, blue for abortion, green for prenatal care, pink for Medicaid information. As I outlined their options and helped them set up appointments, I spoke in the language of the clinic: *Clear, conscious choice. Intended pregnancy. Every child a wanted child.* I liked the sound of these words, the way they seemed to cut through the churning, murky waters of these clients' lives like an anchor, solid and certain. I wholeheartedly believed the gospel I shared in the counseling room: that if we planned carefully and made responsible decisions, we could create the lives we wanted.

Still, I was often baffled by the women's choices. A married woman who tenderly held her squirming toddler on her lap, kissing the top of his head absentmindedly, requested an appointment for an abortion without a moment's hesitation. A schoolgirl dropped her backpack on the floor, rubbed her fists into her eyes, then asked about prenatal care. Day after day, I counseled young women who stared blankly at me through their tears. Whether I was telling them about the adoption process or how to get on Medicaid or how an abortion was performed, I always reassured them that they would be fine. Like a preacher describing the gates of heaven, I relied heavily on my imagination to comfort these women. In truth, I had no idea how it felt to be confronted with such a decision. I didn't even know how to set a clear, intentional course for my own life, which at that time was very much like my surfing: though every once in a while I found myself in just the right place at the right time, and all uncertainty dissolved in the exhilaration of the moment, more often I was off balance, trying to find my feet in a world constantly in motion. Usually I found my feet too late, just as the wave buckled over my head, or I stood up in the wrong place, and the tip of my board took a nosedive, jettisoning me into the water while fifty pounds of fiberglass whipped dangerously close to my head. Sometimes I didn't even see the wave coming until it was crashing down on me.

When my father came to visit, I picked him up from the airport in my car that belched exhaust and smelled of musty wetsuits and towels. I drove him back to my cramped apartment and searched my kitchen for something to offer him, finding only granola, black coffee, and a half-eaten pint of ice cream. As we walked along the beach, he looked into my sunburned face. "If you ever want to do anything with your life, you'll need to move away from the ocean."

I was beginning to think he was right. At work I was tired of repeating the same words day after day to women who seemed to look right through me. I was dating a man whose bed sheets were always gritty with sand and who lived in a tiny beach apartment like mine and didn't own enough dishes to serve a meal for two. While my college friends were continuing their educations or getting married, I was saving my pennies for trips to Baja and Hawaii to surf. I was tired of being broke all the time and building a life around the fleeting pleasure of riding a wave. I decided to apply to graduate school to study journalism, a field that would allow me to indulge my appetite for a good story. When I was offered a scholarship, I gave away my surfboard and drove across the country to the inland college town of Chapel Hill.

. . .

IN NORTH CAROLINA I missed the ocean, but less than a mile from my new house I discovered a network of running trails that snaked through the woods alongside a creek. I ran for miles beneath a dense canopy of leaves, losing myself in the rhythm of my breath the same way I'd lost myself in the motion of the waves. I ran in the early morning, when the woods were nearly deserted except for a tall, dark man, his graying hair cut close to his head, who leapt down the trail like a jackrabbit on long, toned legs. When our paths crossed, he swerved off the trail to let me pass and flashed a broad smile. I began to look for him, to listen for the distinct sound of his gait on the path. We became friendly, and sometimes I wished he would switch directions and run with me for a few miles.

One Saturday morning, just as I reached for a tomato, he appeared by my side at our local farmers' market. A disarming smile played across his face as he lifted the vegetable out of my palm and replaced it with another: plumper, deeper red, its taut skin yielding to my thumb. In California I had only known one kind of tomato: waxy and faded, shaped like a kiwi, stacked into tall pyramids in the grocery store every season of the year. I was used to grabbing a couple from the top of the pile and adding them to my cart without even stopping to examine them. They were all the same anyway: flavorless and mealy. I had not yet learned that a tomato could be read like a book, that if I lifted it to my nose and smelled it like a flower, or pressed my thumb into its flesh, it would tell me a story.

"My name is Ismail," he said, his vowels bent and stretched

by an accent the likes of which I had never heard. Was it Irish? Moroccan? I had no idea.

I nodded and smiled. "I know you from the woods."

"Next time we should run a few miles together."

Caught off guard, I agreed to meet him at the trailhead the following day, though I regretted my choice as soon as I turned my back to him. His obvious interest in me was a weight I didn't want to carry with me down narrow dirt trails. My body knew the work of tending to men like a mother's breasts knew to leak in response to a baby's hunger. Before I even realized what was happening, their need became mine; I smiled more brightly, nodded more enthusiastically, drew out even the most reticent man with probing questions. But that was the last thing I wanted to do during my precious time alone on the trail. I ran to feel free, to become like the deer I often glimpsed through the trees. If he was by my side, I feared I would not be able to outrun the good girl, the polite girl, the bright smiling one who tap-danced across the silence.

The following morning when I arrived at the park that backed up to the woods, he was leaning against his car in the parking lot, smiling. I knelt on the asphalt to lace up my running shoes and we started slow down the trail, making polite conversation. As we jogged past a playground, I commented that I had always feared swing sets as a child: those rickety frames groaning and rocking as children frantically pumped their legs higher and higher into the air. Once, while swinging on her belly, my sister had caught her leg on the ground: her knee had buckled backward. I still remembered how she had howled with pain. He probably thought my fear was silly, I added; all children loved swing sets.

He shrugged his shoulders. "I never played on one," he replied in such a deadpan way that I thought he must be joking. "On the Libyan coast, where I grew up, we made our own swings—from ropes hung between palm, olive, or apricot trees." I fell silent, trying for a moment to imagine a childhood without playgrounds. "Do you have any siblings?" I asked.

He nodded. "My mother gave birth to thirteen kids. Eight survived." He went on to tell me about his younger brother whose nose had poured blood for days—and about the local healer who burned rubber on the fire and forced the child to inhale its toxic black smoke. He told me about the slippery, long leech that emerged from his brother's nose days before he died—and about the daylong pilgrimage his parents made to the shrine of a Muslim saint in a remote village to pray and make an offering so that Ismail would be cured from his own chronic nosebleeds and survive childhood. Swept away by his stories, I lost track of time and distance as we wove through the trees.

As our breath quickened we fell silent, focusing on the ground before us, the pounding in our chests, the burn in our upper thighs. I was surprised by the easy silence between us. We fell into a steady rhythm, running side by side on a path padded with fallen pine needles, sidestepping stones and coiled roots that looked, at first glance, like undulating brown snakes. When the trail narrowed he took the lead, sweeping aside thorny vines before they could scrape my bare legs, warning me about sharp stones underfoot. I stole glances at his long, muscular legs, his nylon shorts clinging to the half-moon of his bottom. After he ran through the gossamer threads of a spiderweb, he frantically swiped at his face, over and over, like a squirrel grooming itself, for the next mile. I smiled to myself, realizing he was afraid of spiders.

When the trail widened we ran side by side once more, and he challenged me by lengthening his stride. We panted and gulped at the thick, moist air, our breath falling into a fast rhythm. He stole glances at my face and backed off when my flushed cheeks and jagged breaths told him it was too much. We sweated and strained, picking up our pace and then falling back, like a dance: I followed as he ran faster, and when I began to slow down he did, too, matching my pace so closely that it would have been impossible to tell who was leading and who was following. The deeper we went into the woods, the longer and harder we ran, the lighter and more fluid I became. The self-consciousness cleared from my head, and all that was left was our breath, the heat of our straining bodies, the pine branches above us gently sweeping the sky clean. At the end of the trail, when we approached our cars and slowed to a walk, a shyness asserted itself once again between us. We were flushed and awkward with a startling new intimacy, achieved without skin ever touching skin.

A few weeks later, a purple bruise spread across the horizon and gusts of wind blew the leaves skyward, revealing their green undersides like flashes of a pale thigh when a skirt catches the wind. There was a hurricane warning. Long lines of nervous shoppers snaked through the aisles of the grocery store: people stockpiled water and batteries or shuttered their homes and made arrangements to stay with friends. I was at home, packing an overnight bag so I could stay at a friend's house outside of town, when the phone rang. It was Ismail.

"Let's go for a run," he suggested in a daring tone of voice. For weeks we had been meeting at the trailhead in the evenings; running with him had become a comforting and predictable part of my routine. I glanced out my window at the street: glistening wet asphalt, swaying trees, a warm wind pressing against the windows. I loved nothing more than to run in a downpour: to explore deserted streets, drenched with rain and sweat; to stomp through puddles in muddy socks and waterlogged shoes. I left my bag yawning open on the bed, slipped off my pants like shedding skin, changed into shorts and a T-shirt, and jogged down the block. We met on a street between our houses, a gust whipping at our faces, and began to run down the middle of the empty street just as the warm rain began to fall. He matched my pace for a while, then darted ahead like a dog let off the leash, tucking his legs beneath him and sprinting for the pure joy of being alive. He doubled back to check on me, then darted out ahead once more. Drenched by the rain, I followed him through town and back to his house, where he promised me a towel and a glass of juice.

We made our way along the narrow shoulder of a busy street. Only a few feet away cars sped through puddles, spraying our shins with mud. Turning down a steep driveway, we crossed the front lawn of a white clapboard house. I followed him up sagging stairs, into a sparse attic apartment whose slanted ceiling forced me to duck unless I was in the center of the room. The tiny living room was decorated with garage-sale furniture and the dark, narrow kitchen could only contain one of us at a time. A faded square rug the size of a bath mat was laid out in one corner. A small bookshelf contained a few books, and along one windowsill, fossils were lined up neatly like a little boy's rock collection. But the room was mostly empty. If the contents of his entire apartment had been hauled out to the curb, the whole pile would have looked ready for the dump.

Poor was the word that came to mind when I looked around at the shabby space—but when he handed me a glass of cold fresh-squeezed juice, and we went outside and sat on the landing to drink it while listening to the patter of the rain on the roof, I realized this was not an accurate assessment. The apartment looked out on a lush green tangle of woods. Quiet and spare, it lacked none of the essentials: fresh food, good books, privacy and natural light. It was just that it contained so little else. Humble and clean, it felt more welcoming than my own rental, where the bed was unmade and the sink was piled high with dirty dishes. Each item in his apartment—the shiny rocks on the windowsill, the clean-swept linoleum and oak floors, the worn bedspread smoothed tight—seemed to glow from his loving touch. Images of my previous boyfriend's spacious home flashed through my mind: brand-name clothing strewn across the floor, CDs precariously stacked on a pricey music system, liquor bottles spread across the kitchen counter. The absence of clutter or excess in Ismail's small apartment made it feel far more spacious to me than much bigger homes.

Seated shoulder to shoulder on the top stair of his apartment, holding our juice glasses, we stared out at the woods. The wet hurricane wind reminded me of ocean spray.

"I miss the ocean," I murmured.

"Me too," Ismail said. I told him about wading into the steely gray Pacific ocean on misty overcast mornings, paddling out to contemplate the endless horizon while the swell of gathering waves rolled gently beneath me. He described the azure water of the Mediterranean that lapped at Libya's barren, rocky coast. He told me about spearfishing along a reef for hours at a time on blistering summer days, returning home only when he had caught enough fish to feed his entire family. He described the dusty road he walked each day to the one-room madrassah where he went to school, and his village's closet-like library where four boys crowded around the same book, waiting patiently to turn the page until each had read the previous one. He told me about the packs of wild dogs that roamed the desert perimeter of his village—how one night they had surrounded his father as he walked home alone in the dark, snarling and baring their teeth. The biggest one had lunged, and Ismail's father had grabbed for the animal's throat, howling and slobbering like a madman and clutching at that matted fur, and when he finally released his grip the animal dropped lifeless to the ground and the rest of the dogs scattered. The world he described was to me as fantastic and remote as a fairy tale. I was riveted.

As he spoke I studied his face close up for the first time, taking in unsettling details I had not noticed when we ran side by side: Fine wrinkles spreading from the edge of his eyes. A receding hairline. Yellow stains on his teeth. I glanced down at his threadbare T-shirt with faded lettering advertising a race from a decade ago. *No,* I said to myself. *No way.* None of the details I took in matched up with the mate I had imagined for myself.

For as long as I could remember, I had understood life to be a game of acquisition, much like the board game I had loved to play as a child. The key to winning the game of Life was to start with a college education, because it meant receiving a bigger fistful of colorful bills each payday I passed on my way to the finish line. The next step, after a short bend in the road, was to get married: to add a little blue peg beside my pink one in the front seat of a car whose backseat allowed up to four children.

Each passing year would bring more: a starter home, twins, a pay raise, a family cruise vacation. I would spin the wheel of chance and count my steps forward, and my life would progress as an unbroken series of expanding opportunities. At the end of the game, when I reached retirement, I would reside at Millionaire Estates or Countryside Acres—each of which had its own distinct appeal. Then it was time to count the money. The one with the most cash always wins.

An older, darker, poorer man was not part of this game—especially not this middle-aged man with his thick accent and tiny apartment he rented for three hundred dollars a month, to which he invited me without a trace of shame or self-consciousness, as if his possessions had nothing to do with who he was. Perhaps this aspect of him felt more foreign than anything else.

The only piece missing from the board game, its past and future laid out in tidy squares, its neat calculation of the dollar value of major life events, was unbidden emotion. When Ismail laid his hand over mine at his kitchen counter, my heart was not troubled by the cheap wood paneling on the walls behind him or the chips in the mismatched cups on the linoleum counter. The heat from his palm passed through my skin and into my bloodstream, then flowed straight to my grateful heart, which received it without criticism or judgment.

Ismail lived alone, but like the boy who made the velveteen rabbit real by loving it until it was threadbare, he brought his shabby belongings to life through loving attention. He slept beneath a worn cotton blanket as soft and familiar as an old T-shirt. He wore a twenty-year-old down jacket covered with carefully sewn patches. He brewed his coffee in a ten-year-old machine, its white plastic streaked brown where steam had scalded it for the past decade. The machine no longer allowed us to pour a cup until the entire pot had brewed, at which point it emitted a phlegmy cough and a long sigh, like an old man clearing his throat in the morning. That sound was our cue to wait a few more minutes while the last of the coffee dribbled into the carafe. Ismail stood in his small kitchen waiting—not while eating or surfing the Internet or occupying himself in other ways. He just stood before the machine as if politely waiting for it to be done speaking. Once he had poured and drunk a cup, he returned to his machine and began to carefully dissemble it piece by piece, like a boy with a model airplane, lovingly wiping its stained surface with a cloth and digging into each crevice to draw out grounds, which would otherwise clog its old arteries.

His bedroom window looked out onto his vegetable garden, which was overgrown with pungent basil, crisp skinny cucumbers and fat red tomatoes. Fragrant pink peonies exploded like popcorn along the walkway to his door. He waded knee-deep into the flowers with a pair of scissors, bent slender stalks gently toward him, and selected three blooms, which he arranged on his kitchen counter in an old glass bottle he had found in the ravine. He had a passion for music and a vast record and CD collection—blues, country, rock, the traditional music of his homeland—but he loved silence just as much.

I spent the night with him. In the morning we watched the sunlight dance over his oak floor. The only art adorning the blank white walls of his bedroom was the window itself: a walnut tree drawn sharply against the blue palette of the sky. When I got out of the shower, a cup of steaming coffee waited for me on the bathroom counter. Chipped paint tickled the bottoms of my feet as I sat out on his porch steps in the morning, letting the sun warm my face. A stillness settled over me. He was like a deep pool into which I dove without a second thought, not realizing how thirsty I had been.

2 | Genie

Soon after we started dating, I began to call Ismail "Turtle." The name slipped unexpectedly from my mouth, surprising us both. He flashed me a bewildered smile, one that said I was a mystery to him—not an ominous one but a delightful one, one he wanted to investigate further. Perhaps he thought the name came from the small, bloodred turtle that sat on the windowsill in his bedroom—a gift from a former student, he told me—the first thing I saw each morning I awoke at his house, with its glossy shell and tiny, bobbing head on a spring that seemed to nod an almost imperceptible *good morning*.

Or perhaps he thought the nickname came from his deliberate ways that made my skin prickle with irritation, and I had to walk away to stop myself from complaining. In the mornings I slipped on my shoes and buckled my belt as I bounded down the stairs, balancing an overfull cup of coffee in one hand. He stood in front of his closet, blinking at shirts buttoned and starched and lined up like a military procession. In the car as

I waited for him I fiddled impatiently with the air vents or the stereo, sighing and peering up at the apartment. I could see him moving from window to window, checking each one to confirm it was closed, then disappearing to wipe down the kitchen counters one last time. When he finally emerged he sat down on his porch steps and loosened the laces of his shoes like a musician tuning an instrument, adjusting each string as if it needed to be in perfect pitch. By the time he reached the car, I had swigged the last of my coffee and was tapping my fingers impatiently on the dashboard.

But his nickname had nothing to do with the turtle on his windowsill or his slow, maddening ways. Instead it came from lazy weekend mornings in bed when he propped up on one arm beside me, and the late-morning sun bounced off his bare white walls, illuminating his hooded eyelids, the fan of wrinkles around the edges of his eyes when he smiled, the folds of skin gathering at the base of his neck. I had never seen the effects of aging on a lover's face. I studied a faint age spot on his forehead like a brand marking him as part of the mortal herd. He spoke tenderly to me, but I couldn't hear what he was saying; my ears were craning for the inaudible crinkle and pop of wrinkles forming, the slow, inexorable slipping of skin down his neck. The *whoosh* of passing time was a distant hum in my ears that I had never heard before.

If life was like a long run down a winding trail, I now had the unsettling feeling that it was nowhere near as long as I had imagined. He was somewhere far ahead of me on the path; all I could see was his receding back as he approached our common destination. Sometimes I felt a sudden panic that I would never be able to catch up with him, that I would ultimately be left alone. When that panic arose on those bright mornings in bed, I turned away and studied the faded sheets instead of his face, only shrugging when he asked me what was wrong. In the shade of the woods or the dim light of a restaurant, he looked young, but on bright sunny mornings he looked weathered, like a sea turtle emerging from the deep, with its mottled shell and leathery skin, its hooked nose and ancient black eyes. I felt embarrassed on his behalf, as if no one had told him that in this culture aging was in poor taste, as if he simply failed to realize it had gone out of fashion.

I had always assumed that the unwritten exchange between younger women and older men was power and security in exchange for sex and youth. The only man I knew with a much younger wife was my neighbor Chuck in California, who had left his wife after falling in love with one of his high school students. The year she turned eighteen she walked down the aisle twice: first to graduate and then to marry her science teacher. On their wedding day Chuck stood beaming at the altar, his full beard already speckled with gray, fine wrinkles spreading from the edges of his moist, hungry eyes, watching her walk shyly toward him in a strapless white sundress. With her pale, skinny shoulders and blushing, plain face, she looked more like a girl at her confirmation than a bride. Her father wore an expensive suit and a pinched smile, and afterward at the reception he and his wife huddled close to one another and glanced around like they were in hostile territory, like something precious had been stolen from them. In a show of masochism disguised as new-age tolerance, Chuck's ex-wife attended the wedding and sat in the back row beneath a floppy sunhat that hid her sad brown eyes. The lower half of her face was frozen into a brittle smile. I remember the very air at the wedding being singed with scandal, like the acrid aftermath of a fire.

Ismail was not old; he was a fit, handsome, energetic man in his forties. But for the previous ten years I had lived in a Southern California beach town teeming with tan, perfect bodies. From my apartment it was only a short walk to the shoreline, where beautiful people preened on colorful towels that framed the glistening bronze artwork of their bodies. Day and night, toned athletes jogged up and down the boardwalk like spandex-clad sentries guarding this oasis of youth from the assault of time, which loomed like a slow-gathering storm cloud in the distance. Every storefront, every magazine, every television commercial promoted a new weapon in the battle against aging—from dieting to workouts to fashion to plastic surgery—and everyone I knew was fighting on the front lines. Our modest paychecks from our minimum-wage jobs were just enough to cover cheap ammunition, and we staked our claim to youth and beauty with the fierce determination of the fanatical.

I had come to see growing older as a weakness of character, an inexcusable slothfulness, a crass disregard for style.

I shared a tiny beachside apartment with a hairdresser, a striking Latina woman named Lorena who had movie-star looks and never missed a workout, whose closet overflowed with designer clothes she'd bought on credit. She took over an hour to get ready each morning, changing several times and flawlessly applying makeup and drying her hair with a roller brush with the circumference of a salad plate. Her boyfriend came to our house to watch football, drink our beer, and tease Lorena for being scatterbrained. When he pontificated about life, she widened her big brown eyes and put her index finger to glossy pink lips. With her lush black mane swept up off her neck, her cocked hips and her doe-eyed stare, she looked like she had just stepped out of a scene from *Breakfast at Tiffany's*. Five years older than I, she warned me of the pitfalls of life after thirty, reminding me that soon I would have to buckle down and get serious about my looks, that my flippant attitude about makeup and hair and diets would no longer suffice. Even though she made it look easy, she told me, it took real focus and determination to stay beautiful.

The littered sliver of coastline where I lived was crowded with bars and surf shops and rundown apartments. To the east it was bordered by the I-5 freeway, which was clogged morning and night with commuters, unfortunate souls who had traded youth and freedom for mortgages and health insurance. Some

of the first cars to pull into the beach parking lot each morning with surfboards strapped to their hoods sported bumper
stickers that read THERE'S NO LIFE EAST OF THE I-5, and this was
exactly how many of us felt. East of the freeway were station
wagons and malls like concrete islands in a glittering sea of
chrome; tract housing developments that ate away the desert
like a fast-spreading virus. East of the freeway were crow's-feet
and receding hairlines, potbellies and polyester pants. East of
where I lived was the neighborhood of middle age, with its
mown green grass and identical houses crowded onto cul-de-
sacs. I never wanted to move inland.

Ismail was not the first older man I had become involved
with. In California I had briefly dated a wealthy doctor in his
forties who had a deep tan, a muscled chest, and expensive
highlights. He filled his sprawling oceanview home with people
decades younger at raucous parties like those I had attended in
high school, except that people passed out on expensive Italian
leather couches instead of in the rusty beds of pickup trucks.
Though he was fifteen years older than me, I felt strangely like
his mother, checking my watch as night slipped into morning,
mentally counting the drinks he had emptied, pursing my lips
in disapproval and flashing him warning looks. He treated aging like influenza—terminal for the indigent but curable for
those with enough resources—and he seemed to have driven
his own aging into remission.

But Ismail was aging differently—as if aging were an epidemic that ran rampant in the poorer, darker parts of the world. As if one year spent slathered in sunscreen, watching the waves roll in from behind a hundred-dollar pair of sunglasses, was equal to two spent spearfishing for dinner for the entire family on the impoverished North African coast. As if he didn't even consider time his enemy.

It made no sense for me to fall in love with this older, foreign man who rented a tiny, sparse apartment in which he collected nothing but old things. He did not have a perfect, muscled body. He did not buy me expensive jewelry or silky lingerie or whisk me away to a hotel to drift through long weekends on bedding as white and pillowy as clouds. But there was something about him that made me feel like I could finally exhale and embrace silence; opening up to him, I was also opening up to myself. It seemed to me I had been running for a long, long, time: achieving, avoiding, learning, growing, consuming. In all my striving I had missed out on one simple thing: the fact of being here, in my body, at this very moment, on this faded bedspread and these worn cotton sheets, with his thrift-store lampshade glowing like the setting sun.

ONE LATE FALL afternoon I lay in his bed watching leaves float by his window like tiny magic carpets. Fingerlings of sun stretched out across the bedspread and our bodies. Stroking the back of my arm, he began to describe the dark, narrow store in the local souk, or marketplace, where his illiterate father had spent each day behind the wooden counter selling goods to neighbors: a deck of cards, a pack of cigarettes, a bar of soap, a bag of rice. Some paid on the spot for their purchases, but most kept a tab, returning to settle their debt when their luck changed and they could afford to. Friends and neighbors emptied items from the narrow wooden shelves and slipped out the door, while Ismail's illiterate father murmured their names and purchases over and over again under his breath and waited impatiently for his son to arrive. Just as the accumulated weight of the day's transactions was becoming too heavy for his tired mind to carry, Ismail burst through the door, threw his school books down, and opened the ledger, pen in hand. His father spilled out an urgent summary of the day's transactions, which Ismail transcribed furiously onto the page.

"Let me show you something," Ismail said, rising from the bed and moving to his closet, where he reached up to retrieve a package from a high shelf. Pulling down the paper-wrapped bundle and laying it on the bed, he carefully unfolded a black *jalabiya,* or floor-length robe. He slipped it over his naked body. His skin disappeared beneath black cloth and shimmering gold thread, and with an expert sweeping motion of one arm, he twisted and wrapped his head in a gauzy white strip of cloth. He turned to face me, a shy, uncertain expression on his face.

I gasped. I had only seen him in American clothing—jeans and T-shirts, shorts and running shoes, baseball caps and fleece jackets—and even then his foreignness clung to him as persistently as the pungent spices that lingered in his clothes. There was always something to remind me he came from a different world: the way his tongue tickled the roof of his mouth every time he made the sound of an *r*, the Arabic books that filled his shelves, whose script looked so much to me like a child's pretend game of writing. His loud, animated phone conversations with his family in Libya, exchanges that sounded to me like heated arguments but which he insisted were only friendly chats. Standing before me in traditional clothing, he became someone I barely recognized. Beneath the brilliant white turban his face seemed a richer brown, his eyes a more intense black. In the robe, with gold thread running in rivulets from his shoulders to the floor, he looked as regal as a prince, more noble and imposing than a man in pants could possibly look. Feeling suddenly exposed and vulnerable, as if in the presence of a stranger, I drew the covers over my body.

"You look like a genie," I said nervously.

He lifted his arms skyward, his fingers fluttering, his loose black sleeves billowing like wings.

"*Shubbaik lubbaik, ana bain edaik,*" he chanted in a low, melodramatic voice, furrowing his brow and widening his eyes at the same time, pinning me in his gaze.

Your wish is my command.

Suddenly the regal Arab before me was gone, replaced by a cartoon Arab, a Disney character on a magic carpet. Now he was a dark bad man in an Indiana Jones movie, part of the hypnotized throng who prayed on all fours to the evil lord of fire, chanting mumbo jumbo and raising their backsides into the air. Or he was the bloodthirsty Libyan hell-bent to slaughter the brilliant scientist in *Back to the Future,* the one who careened through the mall parking lot in a VW bus, his checkered head cloth snapping in the wind as he sprayed gunfire like rain onto the asphalt.

His laugh was contagious. I drew my knees up to my chest and began to giggle, but his spell over me was only partly broken. He was no genie; he was my friend and my lover, and we were laughing together in his small apartment on a late Sunday afternoon. But part of me was still caught up in a feverish dream in which he was a genie sprung from a bottle, whose only purpose was to grant me my heart's desire. He was the tall, dark stranger who with a word or gesture could make me beautiful and happy, make my life meaningful and whole. I had been in search of a savior and dreaming some version of this dream for as long as I could remember, sleepwalking through every romantic relationship I had ever had. I took a deep breath. This time I would take responsibility for my own happiness; all I needed was a companion to join me on the adventure.

3 | *New Life*

I stood in the bathroom of Ismail's apartment, staring in disbelief as a thin pink line appeared on my pregnancy test like a fault line beneath my feet. We had only been dating for a few months. I vaguely recalled having missed a pill or two sometime before, but I had assumed I was protected nonetheless. How could I have been so cavalier about the risk of pregnancy, after having witnessed the consequences of such behavior over and over again? I sat down hard on the cold tile floor.

Ismail was at work. To occupy myself until he got home, I did several loads of laundry at the Laundromat, which was empty except for a slow-moving woman in stained sweatpants and her two children. Her toddler careened around the room, screeching and banging the dryer doors as hard as he could. The baby sat on his mother's lap and stared at me, drool running in rivulets down his chin and into the fat creases along his neck. A green line of snot snaked from his nostrils to his mouth while his mother stared at the linoleum floor.

That evening I told Ismail I was pregnant. He sat down on his couch and cried, whether from elation or dismay I couldn't tell. I sat next to him and awkwardly rubbed his arm. I did not know what to do with a crying man. Later we sat out on his back steps, watching the darkness overtake the woods. He seemed both excited and wary, and he studied my face for clues about where I stood. Mostly he communicated through physical gestures: stroking my back, squeezing my fingers just enough for me to feel his strength but not hard enough to make me feel constrained. He brewed me some tea, and together we watched the steam rise from the cup and disappear into the blue-black sky.

I'd always imagined I would have a child one day—after I'd been married for years and my young, successful husband and I had grown tired of traveling, and hosting dinner parties for our smart and stylish friends. I'd have an established career and a home office where I'd compose thoughtful essays while my parents and in-laws, who each lived nearby, took turns baby-sittng our child.

In my journal, I wrote down a quote from W. H. Auden: "We would rather be ruined than changed. We would rather die in our dread than climb the cross of the moment and let our illusions die."

In the days that followed, I weighed the possibilities over and over. I'd just been awarded a fellowship to work abroad the following year as a broadcast journalist. Terminating the pregnancy would mean I could maintain my independence, travel the world, and pursue my career. Having a baby would mean trading this prestigious opportunity for women's most ancient work: childbearing. I'd be pregnant and unemployed, far from family, possibly a single mother. If Ismail and I stayed together, I'd be raising a child with a man who was fifteen years older than I was, whose small apartment was pungent with strange spices, who spoke so passionately that I often felt he was yelling.

My formerly carefree relationship with Ismail felt suddenly heavy, weighed down by the decision before us. We continued to run along the dirt trails together in the mornings. One day we wove in and out of a dense thicket of scrub pines, falling into single file where the path narrowed, then jogging shoulder to shoulder where it widened again. Without warning, Ismail broke his gait and turned to face me.

"What exactly are you looking for in this life?" he asked, struggling to catch his breath, his eyes searching mine. "Love? Freedom? Family? Adventure?" He raised his voice and swept his arms toward me, palms upward, as if balancing my fragile future in his outstretched hands. "Don't you see? It's all here in front of you. Right here. Right now."

I stared at him. Beads of sweat trickled from his hairline, past the deep wrinkles that framed his intense, nearly black eyes. His threadbare cotton T-shirt, stained dark with moisture, drooped from his shoulders. All around us scrub pines stretched toward the light, their brown trunks as scrawny as children's arms. The thick, damp air clung to me. In the distance I heard the sound of traffic. *This is not how my life is supposed to be*, I thought.

Over the next few weeks Ismail and I stepped carefully across the fault line of the positive pregnancy test, which now divided our past from our future. I dozed off on the couch in the middle of the day and had frantic dreams about finding crying babies everywhere—in my backpack, at the bottom of a laundry hamper, on the floor of my car. A startling heat deep in my middle woke me during the night, and I could fall back to sleep only with my belly pressed hard against Ismail's back, the tops of my feet against his soles. Strange new sensations coursed through my body. My stomach turned at the stench of cooked fish, which hung in the air like a curse for days after we'd eaten it. I recoiled from the trace odor of mildew woven into Ismail's sweaters, the thin smell of decay on his breath. I cried and wondered how I could possibly bring a baby into this rotting world—and then I wondered how I could possibly do anything but that.

ISMAIL TOLD ME that in the North African village where he had been raised, marriage would have been our only option and that men and women had been killed for the offense of conceiving a child outside of wedlock. His casual conversation was always peppered with references to Allah: God willing, the weather would improve. Thanks to God, he had gotten over a cold. But now he held me squarely by the shoulders, looked into my eyes, and told me he would accept whatever choice I made—and I believed him, even though we had been dating for less time than it would take to carry this pregnancy to term.

I knew well what a woman's options were in California, but I hadn't yet familiarized myself with the medical resources in North Carolina. I went to a local clinic, where I sat in a small office with a young woman who popped her gum as she took my medical history. When she left the room to administer my pregnancy test, I could hear her giggling and chatting with her co-workers about her weekend. She returned to the tiny room, her face sober. She outlined my choices and asked me what I wanted to do.

It seemed like such a simple question. On the one hand, I wanted to pursue the life I had imagined for myself. But I couldn't figure out how to measure the value of my goals against the value of this pregnancy. Was an unplanned pregnancy any less precious, mysterious, or promising than a carefully planned one? For the first time I was beginning to wonder whether the pursuit of my own desires was the best strategy in life.

I'd spent so much time thinking about my future, but now I saw that all I had was this imperfect moment: This queasiness. These full, tender breasts. This young woman across from me, with her bright expression. This gentle man in my life, with his musical accent, his warm hands, his tiny apartment. I'd imagined myself as autonomous, but even that was an illusion:

Ismail was lodged in my heart as surely as this new life was lodged in my womb, and I would be able to extract myself from these relationships only by what felt like an act of destruction.

The young woman circled phone numbers on color-coded information sheets, tapped them into a stack, and handed them to me. I was grateful for all the alternatives available and for the fact that this choice was mine alone to make. But I did not feel "empowered." Instead I felt brought to my knees by this burden. I knew that whatever path I chose would lead me first to grief—for the loss of the life I'd planned or for the loss of the life I carried—and that I would have to live with this decision for the rest of my life. Through feminism I'd discovered strength and ambition, but I knew little about the subtler rewards of acceptance and surrender. What gifts might come if I relinquished my expectations of how my life should be, if I submitted to my circumstances instead of trying to control them?

Alone in that anonymous office, I felt a belated rush of understanding of the women I had met in the clinic back in California: the mother who had chosen to end her pregnancy, the young girl who had chosen to continue hers. I understood that sometimes love has the power to drag us under and that there are also times when we have to dive headlong into our fears in order to find our joy. I understood that whatever choice these women made—whatever choice I made—a life was saved and a life was lost.

Soon after that, a strange thing happened. It was late in the afternoon, and I was sitting in Ismail's apartment crying. His eyes glistened as he leaned in toward me from across the table. My exhausted, racing mind paused its endless deliberations, and in his unwavering gaze I saw a love as vast as an ocean. I could see that it was big enough to contain my fears and regrets, big enough to embrace whatever choice I made. In the silence that stretched out between us, I felt my fears begin to recede, and in their absence I recognized different emotions: gratitude for this man and awe for this mysterious new life entwined with mine. Though it would seem crazy to abandon the future I had planned in such a small moment, it would somehow be enough to lead me into a future I'd never intended—or even knew how much I wanted.

MY BELLY, FORMERLY a flat expanse between my hip-bones, grew round as a globe, as if I were carrying within me a whole new world. At night I lay on my back in my underwear, watching new life surface and roll against the soft walls of my abdomen, then dive back into the depths of my body, like the arc of a dolphin rolling between sea and sky. Like a figment of my imagination, I glimpsed the curved ridge of a tiny spine, the round back of a heel, a small, bony bottom. At night I dreamed of the taut skin of my belly tearing like tissue paper against the weight of this somersaulting body, of frantically tucking tiny limbs back inside as hot blood spilled through slippery fingers.

For years I had managed to freeze my body in time, to keep

it as angular and lean as it had been on the cusp of maturity. Exercise was for me like prayer for the devout: a daily ritual that shaped my days, gave me a sense of purpose, purified me. I had trained my body to conform like a drill sargent controls his platoon: demanding total obedience, pushing its limits, trusting without question the purifying power of self-denial and muscle burn, as if pain itself were a form of salvation. Without my strict oversight, I believed my body would never be capable of self-governance; it would collapse into self-indulgence. I had no tolerance for its softness, its languor, its hungers, and as a result it had become strong and disciplined, my weight hovering closely around a single point like a compass toward true north.

But now my body had been infiltrated in the dark, colonized by a new life that toppled my tyrannical regime. My formerly small breasts swelled and lay warm and heavy against my skin, the areolas darkening with newfound purpose. I grew sluggish and dreamy, forgot what I was supposed to be doing or why it was so important to keep moving all the time. I contemplated a pile of unfolded laundry on my bed like it was a riddle I couldn't solve, tried in vain to come up with a strategy for sorting and folding it, then abandoned the project altogether and curled up instead like a sleepy-eyed cat. I ate pints of ice cream straight from the carton, moaned with pleasure when that sweet cream melted across my tongue and slid down my throat. At night Ismail's skin was my security blanket; I pressed my face into his back, greedily inhaling his scent of sweat and soap.

In the past my appetites were like stray cats outside a window, staring at me with recriminating yellow eyes. It was easy for me to ignore them and stay focused on my agenda. But now they scaled the walls of my self-discipline and clawed at me, demanding carrot cupcakes with cream-cheese frosting and thick slices of turkey on pillowy white bread, smeared with mayonnaise and slabs of avocado. Eating was no longer something I could do while driving a car or walking or reading or talking on the phone—like lovemaking, it commanded my full attention, its sensual pleasures obliterating all thought. I was becoming someone I no longer recognized: consumed with desires for food and touch and beauty and comfort, burrowing like an animal deep into its nest.

4 | *Joining the Tribe*

We should get married," Ismail said one night. He lay on his back in the dark, speaking to the ceiling. He spoke matter-of-factly, as if marriage were a durable piece of furniture we should purchase to fill an empty space. Guest lists and honeymoons were not on his mind; instead he was thinking about health insurance and property rights and my protection in case anything happened to him.

Weddings did not hold the same sway over him as they did for me. He had never slipped a wedding dress onto a Barbie doll, then marched her tippy-toed across the carpet beside Ken to a makeshift altar. Nor had he spent countless hours on the playground playing fortune-telling games that pivoted on two questions: whom would I marry and how many kids would I have? He had not sat cross-legged on a carpet in front of a television set, glued to the screen as Princess Diana swiveled her delicate wrist at an adoring crowd on her wedding day.

I was nine years old the summer of her spectacular ceremony. Watching the wedding on TV, I was transfixed by the sight of a horse-drawn carriage pulling up to a cathedral. A princess emerged from a gilded door in a billowing white dress like buttercream frosting, big dollops of white decorating her slender white shoulders. This was no Disney movie; this was *real life*. With her shy smile, Princess Diana tilted her head demurely to show her gently feathered hair. Her straight-backed prince with his broad, ornamented chest held out his arm for her. She put her arm in his, and they turned their back on us, floating away into happily ever after.

As far as I could tell, Ismail was not burdened with fantasies of happily ever after. He had never stood in a tight cluster of women wearing matching, unflattering pastel-colored dresses, laughing awkwardly about the ritual toss of the bride's bouquet, then elbowing and scrambling after it when it was launched into the air. Instead he had tussled over UN rations tossed from the truck that came through his village once a week; he'd watched neighbors walk away with pockets bulging with canned food, while he went home with none. He had gone hungry when a drought destroyed a season's crop, seen young siblings die, and nearly lost his own leg to an infection because he lacked health care. Instead of unspooling fantasies about the future, his imagination produced vivid scenarios of hard times. He knew how quickly life could take a turn for the worse, so he wanted me to be prepared: to have health insurance, own half his home, be protected in case of emergency. For him, getting legally married was as practical as having a first-aid kit in the bathroom.

Every time he suggested marriage I snarled at him like a cornered animal, as if he had just flatly stated I should walk several paces behind him or ask his permission before I leave the house. I had already lost so much control. I had gone from being a single woman with a promising future to being pregnant, unmarried, and unemployed—to spending my weekdays lounging on the frayed couch of his tiny apartment in sweatpants, listlessly watching my body change as if it were a nature show on television. Terrified by the prospect of motherhood, I was still coming to terms with being married to the child I carried. I often woke in a cold sweat from frantic dreams of trying to claw my way back into the past. I balked at losing any more autonomy. His practical approach to domestic partnership seemed tragic. Marriage, I imagined, was about being swept into one's future on a gushing current of love and desire. Instead I was growing heavier by the day, gravity pinning me to this new reality.

BUT HE WAS RIGHT; I *did* need health insurance. At home in the middle of the day while he was at work, I looked around me and realized I wanted this home to belong to both of us; I wanted to claim its oak floors and painted-shut windows, the clover spreading through the overgrown grass, the creaking rocker, and the lazy, swirling fan on the porch. So I agreed to go to the courthouse with him—in secret, just the two of us. I insisted that the papers we signed would not mean anything to me—that only a real wedding, with a dress and a cake and music and a party with loved ones, would bind us.

On a weekday morning we drove to the county seat in Hillsborough, a small town with a sleepy main street and an old-fashioned courthouse. A woman shaped like a wedding cake sat behind a narrow desk: her fair, round face stacked onto her white neck, above a broad, spongy bosom that gave way to a buttercream middle. She slipped forms across the counter for us to complete—boxes to check, numbers to provide, blank spaces to fill in, and signatures to authorize in order for our love to be processed and packaged into legal responsibilities and financial benefits.

After we had completed the forms, she gestured for us to sit down in a nearby waiting area, which was empty except for two young people who looked like they were playing hookie from high school. A blonde girl who had not yet lost her baby fat snapped her gum so fiercely that it sounded like a cap gun. Beside her sat a young man in a baseball cap, the brim tucked low over his face, concealing his eyes. He stretched his long legs in front of him, the knees of his blue jeans the rust color of North Carolina clay, his unlaced work boots crossed over each other. He looked like he was planning a deer hunt for their honeymoon, and they would be leaving directly from the courthouse.

We four sat in silence, contemplating the carpet, glancing now and then at one another with mutual suspicion, like people stuck together in a holding tank at the county jail—stunned at the unexpected turn their lives have taken, waiting to be released from this shame, convinced that everyone else inside is more messed up and dangerous than they are. None of us could have dreamed that our wedding day would look like this or that we would be the witnesses to one another's marriages. I sat brooding under those fluorescent lights, silently interrogating my doubts. This sterile waiting room, with its coarse matching chairs and health pamphlets on the side table, made me feel like a patient seeking a diagnosis and a cure for this love that was wreaking havoc in my life. The stack of paperwork on the clipboard, all those checkboxes I had marked and blanks I had filled in, made my affection for Ismail seem like a loan I would be repaying later with interest.

On a side table, a woman with a black eye and a recriminating gaze stared up at me from a pamphlet, beneath the words LOVE SHOULDN'T HURT in bold, black type. I reached for the pamphlet and stared uncomprehending at those words as if they were written in a foreign language. Love like an anvil had cracked my locked heart open and unleashed an excruciating flow of tenderness. To rise to the occasion of this love was to endure the sting of daily misunderstandings and the terror of this unexpected pregnancy. There was the fear of the unknown as well as the pain of severing from my past and letting go of fantasies about my future. From where I stood, trying to imagine love without hurt was like trying to imagine the ocean without waves: without it, we would be talking about a whole different body of water, smaller and shallower and safer.

I stared blankly at the pamphlet as the final moments of my single life slipped past. Ismail held my hand in his, stroking the back of my palm with jittery fingers.

"Mr. Soo-yah?" Four heads in the waiting area jerked toward the sound of the clerk's voice, which cut through the thick silence like a knife. She peered over her bifocals at us.

"Can you please come up to the desk, sir? I believe you made a mistake on your paperwork."

Ismail looked confused.

"You needed to provide your mother's *maiden* name here, sir—and instead you've provided her married name. Can you come and correct this?" She held the sheet out to him like a teacher returning an assignment to be corrected.

"It's not a mistake," Ismail called out across the room, without rising from his chair.

The clerk shook her head vigorously. "Are you sure, sir? How could her *maiden* name be the same as her married one?" The young couple and I swiveled our heads back and forth between them like we were watching a tennis match.

"Because they were cousins," Ismail replied in a too-loud voice, shrugging his shoulders as if it were the most logical explanation in the world. The young woman beside us pursed her lips and sucked in air as if through a straw. She raised an eyebrow at her boyfriend, who jerked to attention and tipped the brim of his hat back on his head to get a better look at us.

A tense silence filled the room. All eyes were on us. We were like guests on a daytime talk show whose terrible family secret had just been revealed, and now the audience was awaiting the delicious climax of our despair.

I whipped my head around at him.

"Your mom and your dad were *related*?" I sputtered. "Why didn't you ever tell me that?"

He winced at my accusatory tone. "I'm sorry," he turned to me, defensive and apologetic, raising his palms in supplication. "It never came up before."

That was true. So many nights we had stayed up late, plumbing the depths of one another's histories as if mining for gold, greedy for the riches we found there, each tiny, glimmering nugget of connection convincing us we were striking it rich. I had wanted to know everything about him—his dreams, heartaches, his secret longings and nearly forgotten memories—and I had asked him every question I could think of, but not once had I thought to inquire about inbreeding. In the harsh light of this courthouse, with my pregnant belly squeezing against my bladder, poking against my ribs, and compressing my lungs—this suddenly seemed like a colossal oversight.

"It was normal there . . . *Everyone* in our town was related . . . They were part of the same tribe—the Suayah tribe," he fumbled, trying to sound reassuring, reaching out to run his hand down my back. The couple beside us were now leaning slightly forward in their seats. My borrowed maternity shirt rode up, revealing the blue-white translucent globe of my belly, which looked as if it would burst under any more pressure. The minutes stretched out, taut as that skin.

When the clerk called our name again, we went to the window and signed our names on our marriage certificates. "Congratulations," she said with a tight, glazed smile, slipping the completed paperwork across the counter like a barista might slip us a vanilla latte to go. Then she handed me a small plastic bag, which I took without questioning, and we fled out the door.

Ismail and I did not speak on the ride home. I stared out the window at the walls of scrub pines that hemmed in this narrow road. Ismail always listened to public radio in his car, and while I usually objected to its litany of bad news, its droning analysis of the same intractable problems, this time I was grateful for the chatter. This marriage was not headline news; there were far bigger catastrophes in the world than my morning at the courthouse.

Now I was a wife. I had never liked that word—its harsh, whining sound, its implied servitude. Similarly, I had a visceral reaction to the word *nurse,* though I had loved everything about being a candystriper in high school: wearing the pin-striped uniform with the ruffles like vestigial wings at the shoulders; smoothing those crisp sheets tight across mattresses so that the next patient could slip between them like a letter into an envelope; pouring glasses of ice water for patients whose lips were cracked and dry. I liked to linger in the rooms of invalids who seemed to be suffering from a terminal case of loneliness, who brightened in my presence as if my company were the only medicine they required. I loved the sense of being that helpful, that needed—but the word *nurse* made me think of a saintly woman in white making her endless rounds allowing those in need to suckle the life from her. Her nipples might be cracked and sore, her breasts might hang flaccid at her sides—and still the comfort she offered would never be enough; eventually all that hunger would consume her. No, I would never be a nurse or a wife, I once thought—I would never be ravaged by another's demands.

I reached into the plastic bag on my lap. *Congratulations on your marriage!* the leaflet read. On the back side was a business reply card, which I could drop in the mail to receive a free trial issue of a women's home and garden magazine. The bag also contained trial-sized samples of a wife's tools of the trade: a vacuum-packed sample of instant coffee, a single serving of laundry detergent, shiny envelopes of aspirin and antacid tablets.

I saw myself hunched over the kitchen table in a nubby robe in an empty house, after everyone else who lived there had fled the home in pursuit of meaning and fulfillment. I saw myself drinking instant coffee as the laundry machine shuddered in the background, digging through bathroom drawers for an aspirin to assuage the dull ache of missed opportunities. But then I caught Ismail's eye, and he squeezed my hand and smiled. His gaze moved from my crestfallen face to the items in my lap and he began to chuckle, and I could not help but laugh ruefully as well. Back at our house, I tossed my wedding gift bag into the garbage.

5 | *Expecting*

Heaving my eighth-month belly before me, I hurried past the bright storefronts of the mall, holding on to Ismail's arm with my ringless left hand and barely noticing the curious stares of shoppers who looked away sheepishly when they caught my gaze. In our small southern town, we presented a strange picture: a tall, very pregnant blue-eyed blonde in her twenties, led by a balding, dark-skinned middle-aged man with a discernible accent. I waddled on swollen ankles as quickly as I could; I was running out of time. We had driven straight to this mall from our obstetrician's office, after her eyes had widened in surprise during my pelvic exam. "It looks like this baby is coming sooner than we expected," she said. "Do you have everything you need at home?"

She rolled back her stool and peeled off her latex gloves, revealing the largest diamond ring I had ever seen. I stared at her hand, briefly imagining that glittering gem on my own finger, then shot a nervous glance at Ismail. The only evidence in our house that we were expecting a baby was the checkered blue bassinet in the corner of the bedroom, which we had recently purchased at a yard sale. From the moment I had discovered, to my great surprise, that I was pregnant, it felt like we had been scrambling to catch up with reality as it unfolded. I'd imagined we would spend the final month of my pregnancy preparing a nursery, but now it appeared we might not have that time.

"We've got everything we need," Ismail replied with calm conviction, as if he truly believed that all a newborn needed was a mother's milk and a father's gentle hands. "Well, we *are* missing diapers," he added, then flashed me a nervous smile.

"Pick some up on your way home," the doctor said briskly. "Krista's cervix is already dilating; just a few centimeters more and she'll be in labor."

As Ismail drove to the nearest mall, I rested my head against the window and recited a jumbled and increasingly panicked list of purchases we needed to make before my cervix yawned open another few centimeters: a crib and a changing table, a soft cotton layette and a tiny wardrobe, plush animals and hypoallergenic detergent, and a musical mobile to soothe our baby to sleep.

With one hand on the wheel and the other resting over mine in my lap, Ismail tried to reassure me. "We'll be fine—*Insha Allah*." he said, rolling that rhyming, openmouthed Arabic phrase across his tongue, the soothing murmur he added to any statement involving the future. I knew it meant "God willing," and normally I found it endearing, but today it exasperated me. God wasn't going to prepare our nursery; God wouldn't help us pick out baby clothes.

"My mother gave birth to thirteen babies—each time at home—without any of those things," he reminded me. I stared out the window and chewed the inside of my cheek. In the childhood memories he had shared with me from North Africa, the sound of his mother in labor was as familiar and constant as the sound of his Muslim father's call to prayer. He'd told me this one night recently on our drive home from birthing class, where he had stared blankly at the words our birthing instructor wrote in capital letters on a chalkboard: BIRTH IS A NATURAL PROCESS. He'd glanced around at the expectant parents jotting notes on either side of him, then back at me with a baffled expression that said, *What else could birth possibly be?* But he had also told me that his mother had lost one of his siblings during birth, and four more had died in infancy or early childhood—facts that were so utterly incomprehensible to me that I had sputtered "What?" and stared and made him repeat himself.

At the mall, we made a beeline toward the drugstore, where we knew we'd find the essentials we needed. As we passed a jewelry shop, Ismail tugged me spontaneously toward the door. "You need a ring to wear into the delivery room," he announced, squeezing my hand.

Throughout my pregnancy I had insisted I didn't care about

a ring, but when he pulled me toward the glass countertop and I looked down at row after row of glittering diamonds resting on blue velvet, I knew I had lied to both of us. My heart leapt with awe and anticipation, like a child's on Christmas morning. For as long as I could remember, from movies, television, and magazines, I had known that only diamonds reflected the brilliant white light of true love. Over and over again I'd seen images of a beautiful woman's eyes shining with gratitude and awe when a man presented her with a sparkling ring at least as precious and enduring as her own devotion.

It was a stretch to imagine us as beautiful or radiantly happy as couples on commercials seemed to be. Actors on the screen fit together like two pieces of a perfect human puzzle; Ismail and I, on the other hand, kept bumping against one another's rough edges as we struggled to make our lives fit together.

Our relationship had been gestating along with the baby; for these past nine months we'd been getting to know one another in the waiting room of the obstetrician's office, at birthing class, while unpacking the boxes that contained everything I owned in his small home. During these turbulent months, the evidence had been rapidly mounting in my life that fairy-tale endings only happened in picture books. There would be no Prince Charming to sweep me away into happily ever after, only this gentle and maddening Libyan man who was totally committed to the hard labor of making a home and raising a family with me. But a small voice deep inside still insisted that the jagged pieces would fit together if I wore a sparkling gem on my finger.

I scanned the display case hungrily, my gaze landing on a square diamond in an antique platinum setting: not big enough to be ostentatious nor small enough to inspire pity. Its classic setting evoked a certain nostalgia, a purchased connection to the past. Its shimmering white platinum looked virginal, pristine. Everything about it suited me; it was perfect. The jeweler slid the case gently open in one smooth motion, as if trying not to wake me from a sleepwalking dream. Instead of handing the ring directly to me, he placed it suggestively in Ismail's up-turned palm. This was Ismail's cue to act out the longstanding middle-class American courtship ritual.

When Ismail turned to me and slipped the ring onto my outstretched finger, the bright fluorescent lights of the jewelry store turned fuzzy and soft, the water in my ankles seemed to recede, and even his thinning hair seemed to curl with new vigor. I held my hand up to the light and saw an appendage transformed: my fingers slender, elegant, finally all grown up. Ismail was absolutely right: I needed this diamond in the delivery room—more than Ismail's comforting touch, a supportive midwife, or my own deep, measured breaths.

"It's very beautiful," murmured the jeweler in a near whisper, as if it were the face of my newborn.

"How much?" broke in Ismail gruffly, in a voice loud enough for everyone in the store to hear, the voice of a man who was wide awake. The jeweler told him the price. An explosion of air burst through Ismail's lips: somewhere between a cough and guffaw. He fixed the salesman with a broad smile that said, *Let's stop messing around and get serious now, shall we?*

"Listen: I will pay you *half* that, in *cash*, and I plan to take this ring home with me *tonight*," Ismail announced loudly, pounding the glass countertop with his index finger.

Silence fell as the jeweler tried to figure out how to respond. Nearby shoppers glanced furtively over at us, unsure if they were witnessing a negotiation or a holdup.

I gasped, as if water had been thrown in my face. I was painfully aware of the curious stares of other shoppers, suddenly aware, too, of the bloated fingers of my own raised hand in this harsh light, my borrowed maternity shirt creeping up to reveal the orb of my enormous belly and the stretched elastic band of my borrowed maternity pants. In the blink of an eye, Ismail had transformed my glittering fantasy of happily ever after into a nightmare of public shame.

This was not the first time Ismail's bartering had made me intensely uncomfortable. It had happened a few weeks prior, in a cavernous rug store that smelled of incense and damp wool. A Turkish shopkeeper had unrolled a carpet with a flick of his wrist: the perfect size and color for the hallway between our bedroom and what we hoped would become our nursery. Ismail and I had looked from the rug to one another in wordless agreement; this was just the piece we were looking for, at a price we could afford. I turned toward the cash register and dug into my purse for a credit card, expecting Ismail to load our purchase into the car.

I glanced back just in time to see him pat the shopkeeper on the back and ask, with a broad smile, what he *really* intended to charge us for the carpet. The shopkeeper's eyes widened briefly in surprise, and then he smiled at Ismail as if he had just recognized a long-lost friend, even as he began to shake his head back and forth in emphatic disagreement. It was as if both men had stepped onto an invisible stage—their gestures suddenly larger, their expressions more melodramatic. For the next few minutes they hurled prices back and forth—their voices rising in anger, dropping in concession, then rising again in disbelief—until finally, smacking his palm against his forehead, the shopkeeper consented to Ismail's price. He rolled up the rug while I stood behind Ismail feeling sheepish, flashing the shopkeeper apologetic looks and grappling with the temptation to slip him more money. The men loaded the rug into our car and shook hands. Then Ismail gestured toward my swollen belly. "Now what do you intend to give us as a present for our new baby?" he asked casually.

The shopkeeper chuckled, shook his head, and invited us back inside. He dug into a tall stack of carpets, unfolding a small brown rug intricately woven with blood red and fiery orange like the setting sun. He folded the rug and handed it to me with great sincerity and warmth, asking me to promise to return to the store after the baby arrived so he could hold our newborn.

In my family, talking about money, like talking about sex, was considered vulgar. We knew that cash, like body fluids, was exchanged behind closed doors, and we even intuited that these transactions were the unspoken foundation of our lives, but we never discussed them openly—and we certainly never made a spectacle of ourselves in public.

But this time was far worse: he was corrupting what should have been one of the most significant memories of my life—the moment a diamond ring was slipped onto my finger. It was bad enough that I had to witness the purchase; to stand by as he haggled, tossing out numbers and pointing out the ring's flaws, was unbearable. The jewelry store salesman repeated his price. Ismail rolled his eyes and flicked his wrist in the air as if swatting away a fly.

"You've got to be kidding me. For *this* ring? *This* tiny diamond? Come on, we both know how inflated diamond prices are!"

He pulled the ring from my finger and placed it onto the glass countertop with a decisive *plink,* reached for my arm, and turned to leave. Just before we made it through the doorway, the jeweler called after us. We turned around, and he gestured impatiently for us to meet him in the back corner of the store for a private conference. Speaking in a low murmur and

glancing around to make sure no other customers heard his offer, he reduced the price by thirty percent. Speechless, I stared
at him: in all my years of wandering through malls, never once
had I imagined that the numbers on price tags were negotiable.

Ismail nodded immediately in agreement—this was exactly
what he had been expecting—and shook the man's hand. I left
the store wearing a diamond ring that now appeared exactly
thirty percent smaller on my finger, as if it, too, had shrunk in
embarrassment. One day, I imagined, this child I was carrying
might run her fingers over the sharp edges of this jewel. "Tell
me the story of how my dad gave it to you," she would say, and
curl into the crook of my arm, wide-eyed with anticipation of
a romantic tale. What would I tell her about this day? We left
the jewelry store, stopped by the drugstore, then wove through
the parking lot back to our car. With diapers under one arm
and my hand in his, Ismail beamed like a man returning to his
cave with fresh meat from the hunt, like a warrior who had just
protected his beloved from a band of marauders, like a man
who felt that he was truly blessed.

6 | Promises

Ismail was not interested in a bachelor party or a ring for himself or a honeymoon. He had only request: for this marriage to be blessed in Islam.

I peppered him with questions. Would a ceremony have to be done in a mosque? Whom should we invite? What would we wear? He shook his head. It did not have to be done in a mosque—in fact, he would prefer for it to be done in the countryside, in an overgrown field beneath the endless blue sky. His only request was for Surah al-fatiha, the opening prayer of the Qur'an, to be recited before at least two witnesses. I couldn't understand why this was so important—and in fact, it seemed almost superstitious to me—but it was an easy request to fulfill. All I needed to do was stand with him and two friends under the open sky and let Arabic tickle my ears like a gentle breeze. When he offered to translate the prayer, I politely declined, only half joking that as long as I didn't understand it I could not be held responsible for any promises made that day.

We invited the only Muslim couple we knew in town, Jamal and Maryam, along with our non-Muslim friend Jim. My mountain biking partner and one of my first friends in North Carolina, Jim was an investment manager, a triathlete, and a spiritual seeker who tackled the enterprise of enlightenment like it was a start-up company—launching a new practice from the ground up in a burst of creativity and ambition, then cutting ties and starting over when he was struck with a new and better idea for salvation. His dual passions were to make money and to know God. He had piercing blue eyes, a prematurely receding hairline, and an ironic smile, and his strenuous workout regimen made him glow with the luminosity of the enlightened or the extremely fit.

His ramshackle home at the end of a dirt road in the country was covered in Middle Eastern rugs and floor pillows. Mountain bikes hung from the ceiling. When I visited, he invited me to select from a cabinet bursting with teas from all over the world. He poured boiling water from a sea green kettle whose spout was the mouth of a dragon, whose nostrils flared twin plumes of steam. Seated on floor pillows and cradling our steaming cups, we had animated conversations about spiritual teachers who offered the shortest path to God, or concepts for a new stock option he swore would make him rich. On our bikes in the woods, he raced up hills reciting Rumi poems that drifted back to me in fragments, then flew down steep winding trails and skidded abruptly to a halt, dropping his bike and falling to his stomach in the dirt to examine wild ginger plants almost totally concealed beneath ivy.

Jim studied with a a Sufi teacher in town known as Shaykh who had a handlebar mustache, a gray cottonball of a pony-tail at the base of his neck, and a belly that spilled from the ornately embroidered vests he wore with jeans. He and his wife lived in an apartment complex beside the train tracks, among undocumented workers and Burmese refugees, but could usually be found lounging in front of the local health food store, drinking black coffee and smoking unfiltered cigarettes. Each week Shaykh gave teachings at a local hookah bar covered with floor pillows and faded Persian rugs that smelled of patchouli and musty wool. The owner was a tow-ering Moroccan who walked all over town in leather sandals with an ornately embroidered satchel bouncing against his back. Fluent in Arabic, he sat at Shaykh's side, translating his teachings to a hodgepodge crowd that drifted in from the darkened street.

On nights when Shaykh taught, the cafe filled with spiritual seekers with ADD like me and Jim—middle-class Americans shopping for a spiritual path that would offer instant enlighten-ment with no up-front investment. A doe-eyed hippie whose bangles jingled like spare change swished through the door in a floral skirt that swept the floor. Dark-skinned men clustered in the doorway in a nicotine cloud, chatting in Arabic and sucking the last long drag from their cigarettes. A few Muslims would sit straight-backed at the edge of the gathering, looking well groomed, disoriented, and slightly uncomfortable, as if they had showed up at the wrong party. Jim showed up a few minutes after the lecture began because he'd lost track of time while surfing the Internet or working out or engrossed in a discussion with friends over a cold beer in the bar next door. He squeezed in at the front and turned his radiant, tanned face to his teacher, surreptitiously checking his triathlete watch as Shaykh droned on in Arabic.

Back then I thought all I had to do to know God was lounge on pillows with friends, drinking strong, sweet tea, or spin like a dervish in a long flowing skirt. The god I liked best did not require me to pray or perform acts of service, go to the church or the mosque, or change any aspect of myself. It was as if he had given this strange little gathering a special pass, granted us VIP access, exempted us from Islam's tedious requirements of five daily prayers, fasting, study, or self-examination. A few years later, amid rumors of sexual improprieties among Shaykh's close circle, Shaykh and his translator left abruptly for Morocco and never returned. The once-bustling hookah bar locked its doors, and his followers, who had once greeted one another with radiant smiles and long, meaningful hugs, now split into factions—those who believed the rumors and those who did not—and avoided eye contact when they passed one another on the street, like onetime lovers now ashamed of their late-night hungers and misguided vulnerabilities.

On the day Jamal was to read the Fatiha to bless our union, Ismail and I stood in an overgrown field beneath a towering walnut tree. It was spring in North Carolina, the time when trees exploded with pink blossoms and everything green looked as if it had been plugged into an electric socket. Maryam loaned me a gauzy white tunic, pants, and a flowing embroidered scarf. Jamal wore a white tunic, too—buttoned high on his neck, like a chef's jacket—and a black beret which made him look like a French painter. We walked out to the middle of a field and stood beside a towering oak, the sound of traffic humming in the distance. Jim stood beside Jamal, wearing a suit and an ironic smile, his eyes hidden behind wraparound sport sunglasses whose lenses reflected my image back to me, blurry and small.

We stood in a tight circle, the overgrown grass tickling our ankles. Maryam gave me a bouquet of multicolored roses wrapped in brown paper, which I cradled to my chest like a newborn. My hands rested on Ismail's palms—whose warmth always surprised me, as if they were heated by some mysterious source. I had fallen in love with those hands first, before I loved the rest of him, because his touch made me feel like my veins ran with syrup, sweet and slow. Jamal began to recite from the Qur'an, and because I could not understand the words, I listened instead to his baritone voice rising and falling with rhythm and rhyme that fluttered over our heads and drifted away on the breeze. I looked into Ismail's eyes and knew that I could never claim ignorance about this vow; in the bottomless black of his pupils, I read the translation of each syllable that washed over me. No spoken word or written signature was required; my unwavering gaze was my promise.

II | *Foreigners*

7 | *Motherhood*

On New Year's Day, a doctor reached into my abdomen and scooped my furry black-haired daughter out in one palm like she was a kitten. Her tiny limbs dangled from the doctor's fingers as she blinked in the fluorescent light of the operating room, looking as if she'd been rudely awoken from a deep and beautiful dream. I had been expecting the drama of motherhood to begin with a newborn squall, that first sound defining our new roles—her need, my response—but she did not enter this world with a cry. Instead, she blinked and rolled her big brown eyes around the room. Her silence was unsettling; the curtains had parted on motherhood's first act, but the star seemed to have forgotten her first line. I was momentarily frozen, suspended between before and after. She looked as shocked as I was about our comfortable worlds being yanked out from under us.

I approached mothering with the zeal of a new convert, hanging unbleached cloth diapers out to dry in the sun, pressing steamed organic vegetables into ice cube trays, turning up the volume on Beethoven to broaden her tiny mind. I studied the latest parenting scripture and sat in a circle on the floor with other women who had recently been born again into motherhood, having pious discussions while our children played with wooden toys beside us. We were passionate and uncompromising about our beliefs. Co-sleeping, extended nursing, and toddler hour at the public library were holy; baby formula, epidurals, and Disney were evil. We glowed with the certainty of the chosen ones and spoke in hushed and sympathetic tones about the unsaved—those who had not been able to conceive, whose sad stories affirmed our own blessings.

When I was growing up our yellow Labrador, Sophie, had a litter of puppies. The night she delivered her pups, I was awakened from a deep sleep by the soft click of her paws across the linoleum floor. She laid her wet nose on the edge of my bed, nuzzled purposefully beneath my covers, and snorted. She sniffed a pile of clothes on the floor in my closet and then left as abruptly as she had come. The next morning, when I woke up, I found her at the foot of my parents' bed with seven tiny seal-like puppies in a squirming pile beside her engorged nipples. She looked exhausted but serene, and licked her new puppies with a steady, focused intent.

She started out as such a dedicated mother, rarely leaving the basement room in which her puppies were contained. When she briefly left them to eat or to relieve herself, she trotted up and down the stairs like she was late for an appointment, and in response to sounds only she could hear, her head jerked back over her shoulder toward her litter. At the slightest yelp, she'd spin around on all fours and leap like a jackrabbit back in the direction of her pups. But as they grew, her once-lustrous yellow coat turned dull and patchy and her furry brow wrinkled as if she were perpetually worried. No matter how many hours she lay in abject surrender, with her puppies clamoring and biting and sucking, they were never satisfied. It wasn't too long before she growled when a puppy bit down too hard on a raw nipple or snapped sharply at puppies who playfully bit her ears. She stood unsteadily and walked toward the stairs with several puppies hanging from her belly, still latched to her teats. One by one they lost their latch and fell with a muffled thud onto the carpet. Sophie didn't even break her stride.

In the early weeks after Aliya's birth, these memories of Sophie came to me after midnight, when I sat for hours in a rocking chair in our living room, cradling my tiny daughter in the dim light of a winter moon. I was flooded with empathy for the family dog of my childhood: I fully understood her surrender, dedication, and exhaustion. The old hardwood floor creaked beneath the weight of my bare feet, which pressed in a rhythm that slowed gradually until I became too exhausted for even that tiny motion of my toes. Aliya was quiet and alert. I lifted her face to mine, my hands encircling a torso so small that my fingers were interwoven along her back. Her body was a soft, useless weight collapsed into a pile on my chest, but her eyes were luminous. Hour after hour we sat together in the dark, hearing nothing but the occasional exhale of our heater or the distant rumble of a car engine. Her commanding presence filled the empty room: an honored but unfamiliar guest had taken up residence in our home.

"You must be so proud," murmured a friend who stood beside me admiring her pink sleeping face in her bassinet. But I took no more pride in her than I would in a rainbow appearing after a thunderstorm.

Long after the pulsing umbilical cord between us had been cut, we remained closely tethered by a continuous stream of milk and love that flowed from my body to hers. I had an insatiable appetite for her smell, her body heat, the taste and texture of her skin. I curled her into the crook of my arm, squeezed her into my chest, rested my nose on the top of her scalp and inhaled as if breathing in the scent of a flower. "I love you all the way to the moon," I read to her from a book. And then thought: *To the bottom of the ocean, to the farthest reaches of infinity, around the corner into a black hole, and out the other side.*

The first time I left her behind and flew to another city for a work commitment, she was less than two years old. Our impending separation loomed before me, as terrifying as an amputation. I grew as frantic as our dog once did when the door between her and her puppies accidentally swung shut—when she clawed and whined and sniffed desperately at the sliver of light beneath it. But at the airport, as soon as Aliya and Ismail disappeared into the crowd as I made my way through security, I walked through the terminal with a spring in my step I didn't even remember I had. I felt a sweet relief and a surge of energy, as if a large stone had been lifted from my chest. The invisible tether between us slackened, and I leaned into my new freedom.

An hour later, during a layover in Washington DC, I sat in a waiting area across from a middle-aged woman whose graying hair was swept into a tangled ponytail and whose eyes were puffy with exhaustion. Beside her sat a tiny African girl whose skinny legs barely reached the edge of the plastic bucket seat. She wore a pink jumper that was at least two sizes too big for her, and she sat ramrod straight, staring vacantly into the distance with a resigned dignity, like an exhausted, solitary traveler who had a long ways to go to reach home. When the woman offered a sippy cup from her backpack, the girl accepted it without even making eye contact, as if a flight attendant had just handed her some soda and peanuts.

The woman told me she was returning from Ethiopia, where four days prior she had adopted this tiny, stoic girl from an orphanage. After both her parents had passed away, this girl's grandmother had been forced to abandon her at the orphanage because she was unable to care for her. She was two and a half years old. Before they had begun the long journey to their new home, the woman said, she'd spent three days in an Ethiopian hotel room listening to this child shriek and howl inconsolably.

"It was great," the woman said brightly, already displaying that uncanny ability mothers have to extract the positive from even the most trying circumstances. "She rejected me the entire time. From the moment we left the orphanage, she cried—which, of course, was an excellent sign, because it shows she's bonded with *someone* in her life, so she has the ability to bond to a parent figure. I mean, I would *really* have been worried if she'd accepted me from the get-go." Her eyes fell, and she contemplated the carpet.

This pair had been traveling for more than thirty hours already, with many more to go before they would arrive on the West Coast, where her husband and three children waited to encircle this girl as family.

"Isn't she beautiful?" the woman said, reaching over and patting the girl's tiny belly through layers of pink cotton. The little girl stiffened.

"But these curls—I have *no* idea how to take care of them," the woman continued, running her fingers over the child's scalp. The little girl grimaced. When it was time to board the plane, and the woman lifted the child from her seat, she began to cry inconsolably, a haunting wail as if she were grieving the loss of every single face, every single food, every single landscape she had ever loved.

I cringed along with the child when the mother reached out for her, but I was also stunned by this middle-aged woman's courage and commitment, which drove her all the way across the world to collect this tiny, mysterious girl with her unknown wounds, to carry her back across the globe with the crazy conviction that they would become kin. It was an outrageous risk, an improbable act of faith—yet perhaps ultimately not so different from the journey any of us embark on when we decide to become biological parents, when we resolve to stitch our mismatched lives together to make a family.

8 | *Desire*

The first sharp pang of desire hit me in the parking lot of my daughter's preschool. It was a cold winter day in North Carolina, and as I buckled my seat belt another mother maneuvered her gleaming new Volvo station wagon into the space beside my 1992 Honda Civic. She smiled and gestured for me to roll down my window so we could talk.

She was on my passenger side, so I unbuckled my seat belt, leaned across the seat, and groped for the handle to open the window. I rotated the crank, slowly and painfully, counterclockwise. The window jerked down in spurts, as stubborn and recalcitrant as my three-year-old in the backseat. When I had worked my window into its slot, I sat up, brushing away the hair that had fallen in my face. The other mother cocked her head slightly and said, with a hint of awe, "Wow! I didn't even know they made cars like that anymore!" If only I'd had power windows at that moment, I could have coolly drawn a barrier between us with a touch of my fingertip.

Later, at the bank drive-through, I admired how the other

cars' windows slid gracefully open, like curtains before a performance. At night, I dreamed of windows that closed effortlessly, saving me at the last moment from attackers. I became convinced that my manual windows were giving me carpal tunnel syndrome. If only I had a car with power windows, life would be good.

But how would I convince my husband that a new car was an urgent necessity? We had discussed purchasing one when Aliya was born. In the first raw weeks after her birth, when I was too scared even to carry my infant downstairs for fear of falling, I'd insisted we needed a safer vehicle. But Ismail—the same man who went to our daughter's crib throughout the night to check on her breathing and murmur a prayer over her sleeping body—balked at the suggestion that buying an expensive car was part of being a responsible parent.

In the mud hut on the coast of Libya where he had been raised, families collected water from a common well and filtered the larvae from it through empty flour sacks before giving it to their children to drink. By the time he was a teenager, the sound of his mother wailing in labor was as familiar to him as her haunting moans of grief; she had buried five children. Three faint gray lines were visible at the center of Ismail's chest—the last traces of a tattoo his mother had given him when he was a child, slicing his skin and filling the wounds with ash, to protect him from evil spirits. *That* was his health insurance.

In the suburban tract housing development where I had lived in Southern California, we displayed NEIGHBORHOOD

WATCH stickers in our windows and children didn't talk to strangers. Though the names of all the developments rapidly colonizing the inland hills were Spanish, the only Mexicans we children knew of were the ones who migrated north through the canyons, moving in quiet packs in the dark. We knew these Mexicans were real because when we ventured into the ravines, farther than our parents permitted us to go, we sometimes found their tattered blankets and the charred remains of their campfires. We feared these dark, dusty apparitions and made the same mistake as many of our parents did: we confused poverty with evil.

During my pregnancy, Ismail and I had traded tales of our childhoods, captivating each other with descriptions of our "exotic" backgrounds. I described earning my pancake-flipping badge at summer camp; he recalled reciting the Qur'an to a blind imam at the local tribal mosque after school. We reminisced about our first jobs: mine, at Baskin-Robbins at age sixteen, to earn money to satisfy a voracious clothing appetite; his, at age five (for no money at all), stocking the shelves of his father's tiny shop in the village market. We imagined that we had escaped unscathed from the hazards of our respective childhoods and would now build a bright new life together, one that combined the best of American freedom and Middle Eastern tradition. But Aliya upended all those idealistic thoughts.

Some aspects of American parenting thrilled Ismail—such as the first-class university hospital, five minutes from our house, to which our health insurance gave us easy access. But most middle-class parenting rituals mystified him. He could not understand why I spent hours on the Internet, looking up recalls on baby cribs and car seats. He questioned my using hypoallergenic detergent on every cloth item that came in contact with our daughter. He refused to plug in the baby monitor I'd purchased for our small home. When I came back from the store with the entire series of *Baby Einstein* videos, he seemed skeptical of claims about the beneficial effects of classical music on developing minds. He was deeply suspicious of the idea that being a good parent meant making the right purchases; that with enough money, we could protect our children from the pain and ugliness of the world.

When it came to cars, Ismail felt the best way to reduce risk was to drive less, that a good car was one that was paid for and reliable. Both of our vehicles met these criteria. Besides, my husband loved his car. He shook his head scornfully at other drivers, wondering aloud why more people didn't own a vehicle like his. When he was feeling exceptionally magnanimous toward Aliya, he would tell her that maybe, just maybe, he would give it to her one day.

His pride and joy was a 1986 Toyota Tercel. Its paint was chipped, its cracked vinyl upholstery was held together by duct tape, and remnants of bumper stickers from the eighties still clung pitifully to its rear end. I should have taken comfort in his display of loyalty. Instead it annoyed me. When I parked this car amid a sea of Volvo wagons and SUVs at my daughter's preschool, I felt a burning shame.

According to the commercials, a new car came with an overhaul to the buyer's self-esteem—but not for my husband. Looking at his reflection in the gleaming paint job, he saw only a materialistic sucker mired in unnecessary debt. In his mind, to value something that was old and flawed was a sign of integrity. In our consumer-driven culture, which promised to erase all signs of age and decay for a price, it was also an act of defiance. His car had more than two hundred thousand miles on it. Its market value was irrelevant, because he had no intention of selling it. He was committed till the bitter end. When it could no longer exceed fifty miles an hour, he adjusted his driving route accordingly. When the air-conditioning died, he drove stoically through a steaming North Carolina summer. Not even the August heat wave that melted a videotape to his dashboard would make him consider a replacement.

When Ismail talked about his car, his voice softened, as if he were talking about an old friend, one who came into his life long before I did. It made me uncomfortable; Ismail and this car shared a bond I could not completely understand. And I knew that I could never ask my husband to choose between the two of us—if I did, I would be a sorry, lonely woman. But I was not asking him to give up his car. I wanted to replace mine. He listened carefully to my argument. He looked skeptical as I described my parking-lot shame, my power-window dreams, and the repetitive-stress injuries to my wrists. But he could feel the force of my desire. So instead of trying to talk me out of it, he agreed to begin shopping for a new car.

We found ourselves in a vast used-car lot, scrutinizing a mid-sized sedan as if it were a work of art.

"Do you love it?" Ismail asked me. "Because if you do, let's get it."

I walked around the car one more time, trying to determine whether this was the one that would banish my shame and quell my desire. I looked under the hood. I sat inside and examined the interior. It met all my criteria. But nothing about it—not even the power windows—made me feel anything close to love. All I felt was a growing awareness that I was going to get what I'd asked for—and that it would cost me more money than I'd ever spent on a single purchase in my life.

"You decide," Ismail said. "It honestly makes no difference to me." He made a sweeping gesture across the row of cars before us. "All these cars look the same."

My eyes landed on a late-model foreign sports car with sleek lines and a gleaming hood. Next to it, a rusty American car with a crumpled fender bulged out of its parking space. The first auto brought to mind a drive down a winding Tuscan road at sunset, en route to a mountaintop wine tasting. The second screamed claustrophobic American poverty: sitting in a traffic jam on the way to Wal-Mart, the floor littered with fast-food wrappers and cigarette butts. To Ismail, though, they were both just metal boxes on wheels. In that instant, I glimpsed the life-long challenge of our marriage: I assumed we saw the same thing when we observed the world, but our interpretation of what we were looking at would never be the same.

We bought the car. Thousands of dollars, representing years of savings, flew from our hands in an instant, and in exchange I got a used car that seemed safer and smelled faintly of a family I didn't know. On the way home I tested the power windows, watching them glide up and down. In my new car I no longer felt as if I was in exile from the American middle class. I was able to slip unnoticed through the gates of affluence and back into that neighborhood where most of what glittered was borrowed: our houses, our cars, even the clothes we wore. In my rearview mirror I could see Aliya strapped into her car seat, her round face turned to the window, contemplating those speeding metal boxes, the sea of asphalt and steel, the endless storefronts of strip malls. "There are two slaves in a consumer society," writes priest and activist Ivan Illich: "the prisoners of envy, and the prisoners of addiction." In my spacious new car, with traffic pressing in on me from all sides, I felt trapped.

9 | Gifts

Early one morning in September, when our house was pitch dark, Ismail sat upright at the first sound of his alarm, dressed quickly, and left our bedroom. After I made my way downstairs for a cup of coffee, I found him standing at the counter, stuffing the last of his breakfast into his mouth, his eye on the clock as if he were competing in a pie-eating contest at the fair. The minute hand clicked forward, and on cue, Ismail dropped the food he held.

For the next month, nothing would touch Ismail's mouth between sunup and sundown. Not food. Not water. Not my lips. A chart posted on our refrigerator told him the precise minute when his fast had to begin and end each day.

Ramadan is the ninth month of the lunar calendar, the month during which the Qur'an was revealed to the prophet Muhammad through the angel Gabriel. Each year, more than one billion Muslims observe Ramadan by fasting from dawn to dusk. In addition to avoiding food and drink during daylight hours, Muslims are expected to refrain from all other indulgences: sexual relations, gossip, evil thoughts—even looking at "corrupt" images on television, in magazines, or on the Internet. Ramadan is a month of purification, during which Muslims are called on to make peace with enemies, strengthen ties with family and friends, cleanse themselves of impurities, and refocus their lives on God. It's like a monthlong spiritual tune-up.

Fasting was easier for Ismail when he lived in Libya, surrounded by fellow Muslims. Everyone's life changed there during the fast: people worked less (at least those who worked outside the home), took long naps during the day, and feasted with family and friends late into the night. Now, with a corporate job and an American wife who worked full-time, he experienced Ramadan in a totally different way. He spent most of his waking hours at work, just as he did every other month of the year. He still picked up our daughter from day care and shared cooking and cleaning responsibilities at home. Having no Muslim friends in our southern college town, he broke his fast alone, standing at our kitchen counter. Here in the United States, Ramadan felt more like an extreme sport than a spiritual practice. Secretly I had come to think of it as "Ramathon."

I tried to be supportive of Ismail's fast, but it was hard. The rules seemed unnecessarily harsh to me, an American raised in the seventies by parents who challenged the status quo. The humility required to submit to such a grueling, seemingly illogical exercise was not in my blood. In my family, we don't submit. We question the rules. We debate. And we do things our own way. I resented the fact that Ismail's life was being micromanaged by the chart in the kitchen. Would Allah really hold it against him if he finished his last bite of toast, even if the clock said it was a minute past sunrise? The no-water rule seemed especially cruel to me, and I found the prohibition against kissing a little melodramatic. I was tempted to argue with Ismail that the rules were outdated, but he had a billion Muslims in his corner, whereas I had yet to find another disgruntled American wife who felt qualified to rewrite one of the five pillars of Islam.

When Ismail told me stories about his childhood, it was as if he were reading from an ancient, hardbound storybook about an exotic land where the wailing of women was as constant as the howling wind, where children died like stray kittens from diseases I had never heard of, where the thirsty sucked water through cheesecloth to avoid parasites that could colonize the human body and emerge later as worms as long and thick as a pencil. When they were struck with illness, families journeyed for days to Sufi shrines in the desert, where they pleaded with long-dead saints for a cure.

My childhood memories were equally strange and unsettling to him. Like this one: one evening when I was a child, a few days before Christmas, my family sat at the dinner table. I was five, my sister seven. Just as we were finishing our meal, the conversation turned to Santa Claus. What was he doing right now? my father wondered. Maybe putting in a late night at his workshop—and what time was it at the North Pole, anyway? He shook his arm; his watch slid down his wrist. As he was calculating the time difference between San Diego and the North Pole, a booming knock on our front door made us all jump. No one ever stopped by our house during dinnertime.

My dad's eyes grew wide. "I wonder who *that* could be?" he asked, locking eyes with my mother. When he swung the door open, my sister and I gasped: there on our stoop, wiping his shiny black boots on our frayed welcome mat, stood Santa Claus himself, in a red suit so rumpled and worn it must have been around the world and back.

"Ho, ho, ho!" he bellowed, his voice ricocheting off our living room walls.

It was an awkward introduction, but my mother, who is a master at making other people comfortable, took it in stride. She smiled pleasantly as she stood up from the table. "Hello, Santa, would you like to come in?" As if Santa were our neighbor stopping by to borrow an onion instead of a global celebrity who held the desires of children everywhere in the chubby palm of his hand.

Santa waddled across the room and heaved himself into my dad's favorite chair. Patting his thigh, he gestured for me and my sister to come to him. I looked down at the half-eaten meal on my plate and then back at him. Before he arrived I would have given anything for a one-on-one consultation, but now

I wasn't so sure. He had massive, candy-apple red felt arms, bloodshot eyes, and a wiry beard that was yellow at the edges and slid up and down his face when he spoke.

Hovering close together just beyond reach of his broad, hairy hands, my sister and I nervously recited the list of everything we wanted for Christmas. Then I turned to the window, scanning our front yard for that reindeer with the glow-in-the-dark nose and all the rest of them. All I saw were our own toys scattered across our overgrown front lawn. My neighbor's car rolled slowly into his driveway, tires crunching over gravel, the engine shuddering and sighing to a halt in the garage. There was no sign of a sleigh anywhere. Santa explained that he'd left his reindeer at the gas station around the corner. "For a fill-up," he added, with a chuckle and a wink. He *did* smell faintly of gasoline. He wagged his finger at us and told us to be good, and after my mother had taken a few pictures, he disappeared as abruptly as he had arrived.

After I told Ismail this story, he was disturbed and full of questions. Who *was* that man in your living room? What was it like to place your faith in an obese man in a furry red suit? The whole idea of Christmas as a day of reckoning for children, and salvation as a pile of presents beneath the tree, made him anxious. He knew Christmas was important to me, but he had no idea why. He could sense that the stakes between us grew high during the holiday season, so he decided to proceed very cautiously.

"I'm happy to celebrate Christmas with you—please just explain to me what it means to you and how to honor the occasion."

He spoke reverently, as if Christmas were a sacred holiday—and it was, but not in the way he imagined. The high stakes of the season had nothing to do with the afterlife and everything to do with the real and immediate possibility of our home turning into a living hell if he failed to embody the so-called Christmas spirit. Everything depended on his ability to access that elusive state. So he tackled the problem like a scientist, believing that once he could identify its elements and composition, he could reproduce it at will. But the Christmas spirit could not be reduced to a laboratory experiment or a mathematical formula; nor did it lend itself easily to a clear definition.

It had to do with a cut tree in the center of our living room, its branches bent under the weight of ornaments and blinking lights, its trunk girdled with brightly wrapped presents; velvety, oversized socks hanging from the mantel and weighed down with chocolate or mints or bars of soap. It had to do with a particularly flattering family photo, signed and mailed to friends and family; a reindeer with an electrified red nose and a lawn covered in colorful lights. But these elements, however essential, were not enough to make the holiday successful. A twinkle in the eye, a generous impulse, a burst of good cheer were required. If it was difficult to remain in good spirits while fasting during Ramadan, it was exponentially more so to remain cheerful during the Christmas season, in the mad rush of shopping and wrapping and baking and decorating and recovering from a hangover and mailing and receiving and thanking and returning for store credit.

Having always been surrounded by people who celebrated them the same way I did, I had never thought too much about holidays. I had never imagined I would have to explain the significance of chocolate bunnies that laid caramel eggs in nests of shredded green plastic each Easter, or the blazing smile of the jack-o'-lantern on Halloween, or the tree that rained dry green needles onto the living room carpet each December. Each time he posed a question, I felt a sharp loneliness. Explaining these rituals was not easy—especially to such a serious student as Ismail, so eager for symbolism and meaning, so quick to assume that holidays had something important to do with God or history or nature. It was difficult for him to understand holidays untethered from meaning and drifting in an ocean of desire and delight.

I quickly discovered that nothing squashed the Christmas spirit more quickly than the question *why*. The *how* was so much easier to explain: how to strap a tree to our car with bungee cord and soak its trunk in ginger ale so it would stay fresh in our living room; how to pierce the fattest part of a piece of popcorn, thread it onto string, and drape it from needly branches; how to tuck the highest tip of the tree beneath the frilly skirt of a glowing angel. But *why*? Each time he asked this question, my mind was as blank as a desert. Searching that stark landscape for a grain of significance, I glimpsed for the first time an ominous cloud in the distance, the remote and unsettling possibility that my rituals had no meaning.

Like a closely choreographed dance, Ramadan was tethered so tightly to tradition that it allowed no room for creativity. My holidays, on the other hand, were amenable to improvisation. To raise the stakes of our annual Easter egg hunt, my father brought out a stopwatch and timed us like it was an Olympic sprint; Thanksgiving had become the day for our annual bean bag toss tournament. More recently, my family had constructed a new Christmas ritual: the annual gift drawing. A month before Christmas my parents drew names of each relative from a hat. Shortly thereafter we received an email (subject line: Ho Ho Ho) informing us of the person for whom we would play Santa that year.

To have one's name in the hat was to be officially embraced as a member of the family. But failing to grasp the honor and symbolic weight of being included, Ismail only dreaded participating in such a baffling ritual. Each year I had to calm him down and outline the procedure for him all over again. Step one: call or email the person whose name he had selected—my acupuncturist aunt in Santa Barbara, my younger sister's boyfriend with the tattoos and the penchant for pit bulls, my father who had returned or exchanged every gift he had received since 1980. The purpose of step one was to obtain as much information as possible about what this person wanted. Brand names, colors, and sizes were ideal. Just pretend you are Santa bouncing their inner child on your knee, I told him. This only made him more confused.

The level of detail gathered in step one made step two—the purchase—that much easier. A thorough interview could save additional trips to the mall or, if one was shopping online, shave down the process from five minutes to two and a half. Simply enter key words into Google, browse through options, and then click Pay Now (not forgetting to select the gift wrap and personalized card options). The most important part of all was to remain at all times, from start to finish, in the Christmas spirit.

The hardest part for Ismail was not giving a gift but receiving a call from his personal Santa Claus—who was not calling from the North Pole but from the college town where she was working two jobs in order to put herself through school or from the home she would soon lose to foreclosure. Well-meaning relatives called to ask what he longed for, and when he replied honestly that he didn't want anything, they sent him a fleece jacket nearly identical to the one that hung in his closet or a sweater that hugged him a little too tightly around the middle.

"Can't we all just go out and buy ourselves something each Christmas?" he asked me more than once—a question to which I didn't even bother responding. Instead I just flashed him a withering look that said, *I don't know where the hell you left your Christmas spirit, buddy, but you'd better find it fast.*

I SHOULD HAVE been more sympathetic, since I found it nearly impossible to capture the "Ramadan spirit" during Ismail's monthlong fast. People said that for a relationship to work, a couple needed to have a shared passion. My husband and I did have one: food. Years ago, when we first met, we shared other passions, such as travel, long runs on wooded trails, live music. But now that we had a small child, those indulgences had fallen by the wayside. No matter how busy our lives became, however, we had to eat. On days when it seemed we had nothing in common, when I struggled to recall what brought us together in the first place, one good meal could remind me. Ismail was an amazing cook. I could still remember in great detail the meal he prepared for me the first night we spent together: the walnuts simmering slowly in the thick, sweet bloodred pomegranate sauce; the chicken that slipped delicately away from the bone, like silk falling from skin. The next morning the scent of coriander ground into strong coffee filled his small apartment as he served me olives and fresh bread for breakfast.

But during Ramadan, our relationship became a bland, lukewarm concoction that I found difficult to swallow. I was not proud of this fact. Despite the amorphous nature of my holiday celebrations, I did try to maintain a spiritual practice: I stumbled out of bed in the dark most mornings and meditated in the corner of our room with my back to him, trying to find that bottomless truth beyond words. Once in a great while, I dragged him to church on Sunday. Whenever I suggested we say grace at the table, he reached willingly for my hand, and words of gratitude flowed easily from his mouth. He never criticized my practices, even when they were wildly inconsistent or contradictory. But Ramadan was not ten minutes of meditation or an hour-long sermon; it was an entire month of deprivation. Ismail's god was the old-fashioned kind, omnipresent and stern, uncompromising with his demands. During Ramadan this god expected him to pray on time, five times a day—and to squeeze in additional prayers of forgiveness as often as he could. My god would never be so demanding. My god was a flamboyant and fickle friend with a biting wit who liked a good party. My god was transgendered and tolerant to a fault; he/she showed up unexpectedly during peak moments, when life felt glorious and synchronous, then disappeared for long stretches of time.

But Ramadan left little room for dramatic flair. There was no chorus of voices or public celebration—just a quiet and steady submission to God in the privacy of one's home. For some Muslims who lived in the West, the holiday became even more private, since their friends and colleagues were often not even aware of their fast.

During the early days of Ramadan, Ismail dealt with his hunger by planning his next meal and puttering around the kitchen. In the last half hour before the sun set, he rearranged the food in our refrigerator or wiped down our already-clean counters. At night in bed, as I drifted off to sleep, he reviewed each ingredient in the baklava recipe he intended to make the following evening. "Do you think I should replace the walnuts with pistachios?" he whispered. In the middle of the workday, when I called his cell phone, I heard the beeping of a cash register in the background. He was wandering the aisles of our local grocery store. "I needed to get out of the office," he said matter-of-factly, as if all men escaped to the grocery store during lunch.

The last hours before he broke his fast were the most volatile time of day for him. Coincidentally, they were the same hours at which I returned home from work. I'd open the door and find him collapsed on the couch, exhausted, our children, Aliya and a son who was born five years later, Khalil, running in circles around the room. Ismail was irritable, and his thoughts trailed off in midsentence. I dreaded seeing him in this state. I counted on my husband to speak coherently, to smile on a regular basis, and to enjoy our children. This humorless person on my couch was no fun. Every few days I asked (with what I hope sounded like innocent curiosity) what he'd learned from his fast so far. I knew this was an unfair question. How would I feel if he poked his head into our bedroom while I was meditating and asked, *How's it going? Emptied your mind yet?*

One balmy Saturday in the middle of Ramadan, we went to hear an outdoor lecture by a Sufi Muslim teacher who was visiting from California. The teacher sat cross-legged under a tree on a colorful pillow while the sun streamed down on him through a canopy of leaves. After a long silence, he swept his arms in front of him, a beatific expression on his face, and reminded us to notice the beauty that surrounds us. "If you don't," he says, "you're not fasting—you're just going hungry."

I took a sidelong glance at Ismail. He was looking very hungry to me these days. I guess I imagined that during his fast a new radiance would emanate from him. I imagined him moving more slowly but also more lovingly. I imagined a Middle Eastern Gandhi, sitting with our children in the garden when I got home from work. In short, I imagined that his spiritual practice would look more . . . well, *spiritual*. I didn't imagine the long silences between us or how much his exhaustion would irritate me. I didn't imagine him leaping out of bed in a panic, having slept through his alarm, and running downstairs to swallow chunks of bread and gulp coffee before the sun came up. I didn't imagine his terse replies to my attempts to start a conversation, or his impatience with our children.

Ismail told me that in the Middle East, Ramadan was a time of extremes: There were large celebratory gatherings of family and friends at night, and there was also a tremendous public outpouring of charity and generosity to those in need. At the same time, the daytime streets became more dangerous, filled with nicotine and caffeine addicts in withdrawal. People stumbled through the morning without their green or black tea, normally drunk so dark and thick with sugar that it left permanent stains even on young people's teeth. Desperate smokers who lit up in public risked being ridiculed or even attacked by strangers. The streets reverberated with angry shouts and car horns, and traffic conflicts occasionally escalated into physical violence.

Our home, too, became more volatile during Ramadan. Ismail's temper was short; my patience with him ran thin. I accused him of being grumpy. He accused me of being unsupportive. I told him he was failing at Ramadan, as if it were some sort of exam. I didn't ask for this spiritual test, I told him. As if I could pick and choose which parts of him to take into my life. As if he were served up to me on a plate, and I could push aside what I didn't care for—his temper, his self-pity, his doubt—and keep demanding more of his delicious tenderness.

And then there was my husband's unmistakable Ramadan scent. Normally I loved the way he smelled: the faint scent of soap and laundry detergent mixed with the warm muskiness of his skin. But after a few days of fasting, Ismail began to smell *different*. Mostly it was his breath. The odor was subtle but distinct and persisted no matter how many times he brushed or used mouthwash. When I got close to him, it was the first thing I noticed. I did a Google search for "Ramadan and halitosis." This, I learned, was a common side effect of fasting—so common that the prophet Muhammad himself even had something to say about it: "The smell of the fasting person's breath is sweeter to Allah than that of musk." Allah may have delighted in this smell, but I didn't. In bed at night I no longer rested my head on his chest. I began to avoid eye contact and increase the distance between us when we spoke. I no longer kissed him on impulse in the evening. I slept with my back to him, resentful of this odor, which hung like an invisible veil between us.

The purpose of fasting during Ramadan was not simply to suffer hunger, thirst, or desire but to bring oneself closer to *taqwa*: a state of sincerity, discipline, generosity, and surrender to Allah, the sum total of all Muslim teachings. When, in a moment of frustration, I grumbled to my husband about his bad breath, he responded in the spirit of *taqwa*. He listened sympathetically and then apologized and promised to keep his distance. He offered to sleep on the couch if that would make me more comfortable. He said he wished I had told him earlier so he could have spared me any discomfort. His humility caught me off guard and suddenly made my resentment absurd.

Ramadan revealed to me the limits of my compassion. I recalled a conversation I had with Ismail in the aftermath of September 11, 2001, when the word *jihad* often appeared in news stories about Muslim extremists who were hell-bent on destroying the United States. According to Ismail, the prophet Muhammad taught that the greatest jihad, or struggle, of our lives is not the one that takes place on a battlefield but the one that takes place within our hearts—the struggle, as I understood it, to manifest humility, wisdom, and compassion. Ramadan threw me into my own accidental jihad, forcing me to wrestle with my intolerance and self-absorption. And I had been losing ground in this battle, forgetting my husband's intentions and focusing instead on the petty ways I was inconvenienced by his practice.

I thought I understood the rules of Ramadan: the timetable on the refrigerator, the prohibitions, the prayers. But I didn't understand that the real practice was responding to a toddler's temper tantrum or a wife's hostile silence when you hadn't eaten or drunk anything in ten hours. I was like one of the children of Israel in the Bible who once complained that, despite their dutiful fasting, God *still* wasn't answering their prayers. The children of Israel had it all wrong: God didn't count calories. The fast itself only set the stage. God was interested in our behavior and intentions *while* we were hungry. Through his prophet Isaiah, God gave the children of Israel a piece of his mind: "Behold, in the day of your fast you seek your own pleasure, and oppress all your workers. Behold, you fast only to quarrel and to fight and to hit with a wicked fist. Fasting like yours this day will not make your voice to be heard on high" (Isaiah 58:3–4).

Ramadan was meant to break our rigid habits of overindulgence, the ones that slipped into our lives as charming guests and then refused to leave, taking up more and more space and stealing our attention away from God. And it wasn't just the big addictions that grabbed us by the throat—alcohol, coffee, cigarettes—but the little ones that took us gently by the hand and led us stealthily away from the truth. I began to notice my own compulsions, the small and socially acceptable ones that colonized my day: The way I depended on regular exercise to bolster my mood. The number of times I checked my email. The impulse to watch a movie with my husband after our children were in bed rather than let the silence envelop us. And the words: all the words in books, in magazines, on the computer; words to distract me from the mundane truth of the present. I began to notice how much of my thinking revolved around what I would consume next.

I was plump with my husband's love, overfed by his kindness, yet I still treated our marriage like an all-you-can-eat buffet, returning to him over and over again to fill my plate, as if our vows guaranteed me unlimited nourishment. During Ramadan, when he turned inward and had less to offer me, I became indignant. I wanted to make a scene. I wanted to speak to whoever was in charge, to demand what I thought was promised me when I entered this marriage. But now I wondered: was love an endless feast, or was it what people managed to serve one another when their cupboards were bare?

In the evening, just before sundown, Ismail arranged three dates on a small plate and poured a tall glass of water, just as the prophet Muhammad and his companions did long ago. Then he sat down next to me at the kitchen counter while I thumbed through cookbooks, wondering what to make for dinner. He waited dutifully while the phone rang, while our daughter practiced scales on the piano or sent a box of LEGOS crashing onto our wood floor. At the moment the sun set, he lifted a date to his mouth and closed his eyes.

RAMADAN WAS THE time of year when Ismail slowed his relentless forward momentum. While fasting he no longer had the energy for strenuous workouts, impassioned political discussions, or ambitious weekend errands across town. His movements grew more deliberate and his daily rhythm more circular, aligned with the sun and the moon. He spent more time in silence, doling out words a few at a time like dates on a plate.

To his dismay, Christmas affected me in exactly the opposite way. As November days ticked past like seconds on a stopwatch, and December days began their freefall straight toward Christmas, I grew increasingly frantic. At night, after the kids were in bed, I sat at the kitchen counter puzzling over my gift list, racking my brain to try to remember whom I had forgotten, doing the complicated math of trying to ensure that my gifts were precisely equal. I sat up late clicking through our digital archives for a family photo suitable for a holiday card, rejecting one sweet captured memory after another because one or more of us did not look happy or young or fit or successful enough.

One night Ismail lay in bed, chin propped in his hands, watching me where I sat cross-legged on the bedroom floor, surrounded by shopping bags, wrapping paper, gift boxes, and ribbon. I was wrapping my recent purchases in holiday gift paper: tiny ecstatic Santas soared through a glittering blue sky like planes over an airport during rush hour.

"What part of this holiday do you love the most?" he asked suddenly.

I glanced up at him, then let my gaze fall onto the scraps around me. I searched for a better answer than the word that leapt to my mind: *presents*. The unparalleled pleasure of holding a gift with my name on it, the shimmering dream that within bright paper and pretty bows I would find an offering big enough to fill the emptiness inside, that deep, deep hole of restlessness and want. For a brief moment with a gift in my hands, the ribbon still intact and the paper untorn, I forgot what inevitably followed: the relentless creeping desire for something shinier, bigger, newer; delight turning once again to dissatisfaction.

It wasn't just receiving gifts that thrilled me; wrapped up in giving them was a different promise of salvation. Each time I shopped for a loved one I could almost taste that tantalizing possibility of finding just the right object to convey my feelings: to express what I had been too cowardly to say; to erase the memory of times when I had spoken too much or listened too little; to bridge emotional, geographic, or philosophical distance; to make our relationship brand new again.

After having witnessed Ismail's holy month of discipline and deprivation, having seen the way a glass of tap water or a bite of one wrinkled date transported him to ecstasy at the end of a day of fasting, I was too embarrassed to tell him this. So instead I recited something about family and friends, gratitude and good food. I was as credible as the job applicant who brightly insists she is a team player.

The only time of year Ismail was accustomed to giving presents was Eid, the celebration at the end of Ramadan. People came together for feasts and presented gifts to children only—as if brightly wrapped surprises were a youthful indulgence, outgrown in maturity like make-believe games. It made me sad to imagine all the inner children trapped in the hearts of Muslim grown-ups—desperate for scraps of frivolity, longing for reprieve from all that earnest goodness. Christmas, I explained to Ismail, was a time to indulge my inner child: that exuberant, impulsive girl who refused to grow up, whose heart leapt at the sight of blinking holiday lights. She anxiously scanned the presents beneath the tree on Christmas morning, even as I appeared to sit disinterestedly on the couch with puffy eyes and morning frown lines, cradling my cup of coffee as if a caffeine fix were all I wanted from Santa Claus. I liked to imagine my inner child as playful and spontaneous, full of rosy-cheeked wonder at the world. I wished Ismail would be charmed by her, find her irresistible and delightful to please. But he found her demanding and self-centered, and during Christmastime, when she screamed *mine* and *more,* she made Ismail intensely uncomfortable.

Having grown up the eldest of eight children in a poor family, having grieved the deaths of his siblings, and having worked at his father's small shop from such a young age, Ismail didn't have an inner child. Instead he had an inner crone, a wizened sage whose sharp voice had been ringing in his ears for as long as he could remember. She sat cross-legged on a dirt floor in the shack of his heart, chastising him and reciting from the Qur'an she clutched with bony fingers. *Be humble. Work hard. Never forget your obligations to God, family, and community.* She cared less for his happiness than for him to be noble and good and prepared for the trials to come. She fretted over all the temptations Ismail faced in the land of plenty; she knew self-indulgence and suffering went hand in hand.

BY MID-DECEMBER, OUR cul-de-sac was lit up like a silent carnival. During our nighttime walks, a plump glowing penguin in green and red ear muffs waved at us from beneath a tree caught in a web of rainbow lights. On our neighbor's lawn a nutcracker stood stiff and tight-lipped beside a fat Santa in red uniform, his hand raised in a military salute. A reindeer with a coat of flickering white lights grazed on a patch of pebbles. Each evening at dusk, a ten-foot-tall snowman puffed up and rose to preside over the entire cul-de-sac, fat arms raised like a conductor, seams stretched with hot air. Unplugged each morning, he crumpled to the ground, his deflated plastic stretched over the shrubs like shedded skin. Each time I passed his collapsed shell,

I felt a surge of recognition. I sympathized with his dramatic mood swings; this season affected me exactly the same way. The closer the holidays came, the more my mailbox and inbox were clogged with competing offers: Christmas Countdown! Shop Now! Free Shipping! It always happened this way: the pressure built and built until finally, deflated and exhausted, I collapsed into paralysis and dread.

A few days before Christmas, I sat on the couch with Ismail after our children were in bed, admiring our tree. We were curled under a heavy cotton afghan in the dim glow of rainbow lights, and he cradled my bare feet in his warm hands. Every single Christmas we had celebrated together, I had failed in my efforts to surprise and delight him with the perfect present. There was the year of the super-hero underwear, which I later found tucked into the bottom of the garbage; the cap I had knit that was too short to cover his ears; the scarf I had made that fell nearly to his knees.

But this year I had finally found the perfect gift for a man who hated clutter but was electrified by music: two tickets to see his favorite rock band. Why had it taken me so long to think of this? The tickets were sealed into a simple envelope and tucked into one of the two velvet stockings hanging on the mantel, upon which I had paid a local tailor to embroider the names Ismail and Aliya. I'd slipped into his tiny shop off the main street of town just before closing time. He was counting cash from the register; he barely looked up as

I described to him what I needed. A grunt and a slight nod of the head told me he could do the work. He did not look up until I recited the two names. Then he cocked his head, stared, and slid a paper and pen across the counter for me to write them down.

"What kind of names are those?" he'd mumbled, more to himself then me. When I told him my husband was from North Africa, he seemed to take me in.

"Your husband's from Africa?"

I nodded.

"Is he African like me or African like Osama bin Laden?"

I took in his mahogany skin and broad nose spreading across his round face. In my mind's eye I saw bin Laden's narrow coffee and cream profile beneath a white turban, the lower half of his face hidden in a black beard streaked with gray. I wished for a third option.

"Umm . . . perhaps somewhere smack in the middle?" I'd shrugged my shoulders, and he had laughed and shaken his head.

Now the stockings, labeled in script that curled like ribbon, were bulging with small offerings. The following morning, I knew, I would place Ismail's stocking in his lap, and he would smile uncertainly up at me when I encouraged him to reach inside. This year would be different: his face would transform from halfhearted indulgence, to wonder, to real excitement when he discovered the concert tickets.

"You'll never guess what I got you this year," I told him. Smiling, he continued to knead my feet like bread dough.

"Just try," I persisted. "I dare you." I was so caught up in my own excitement that at first I didn't even notice his hands stop moving and his expression turn anxious. When I finally noticed his furrowed brow, I asked him what was wrong.

"I'm worried you'll be disappointed with what I got you." He glanced down at his watch, as if contemplating the possibility of a late-night sprint to the mall. "I'm afraid I didn't get you enough presents."

"That's it! That right there! Do you feel it?"

He looked quizzically at me.

"Feel it? That restlessness in your gut—that frantic impulse to dash to the store, to buy presents you're not sure you can afford or your loved ones will even want? That niggling fear of disappointing those you love, of being disappointed yourself?"

He nodded.

"*That* is the Christmas spirit."

AS MUCH AS I loved them, I could no longer deny that suffering was often wrapped up in the presents I gave or received: disappointment with the wrong gift, resentment for the wrong reaction, shame for forgetting an occasion or neglecting to send a thank-you card, the persistent loneliness of feeling overlooked or misunderstood. As we sat together in silence in the dim glow of the Christmas lights, I recalled our most recent

Valentine's Day. Ismail had pushed the door open with his foot and walked in cradling a dozen red roses, bundled in candy apple red crepe paper and tied up with a pink satin bow. He handed me a small black box which I opened to find the most exquisite chocolates I'd ever seen: ebony hearts wrapped in a web of pink filaments, dense chocolate squares topped with sea salt like cut glass, a pyramid of black chocolate with a pure white tip that drizzled espresso cream over my tongue. I was amazed; for Ismail to offer such traditional Valentine's gifts, I knew, was as much an act of surrender as putting his forehead to the ground in prayer. I knew how much he dreaded this day, when American men circled grocery-store flower displays like sharks or grabbed heart-shaped chocolate samplers from the shelves of drug stores in a distracted rush. So many previous Valentine's Days had ended in tears and anger, when he had refused to participate in rituals he was certain were cooked up by the marketing teams of chocolate and flower conglomerates.

The moment I saw the gifts he carried, I was overcome with guilt.

"I didn't get you anything for Valentine's Day this year," I blurted. Even as I spoke the words, I cringed at how thoughtless they sounded, knowing how hurt and angry I had been when the tables were turned.

I had never done this before. It wasn't that I had forgotten or that I was trying to make him pay for previous oversights.

Twice, in fact, I had gone shopping for him. I'd wandered through sports stores and men's departments, fingered the collar of men's sweaters, sprayed men's cologne in a fine mist on my wrist, loosened the caps on organic shaving creams to sniff them. Argyle socks, belts, pajamas, briefs and boxers—I'd considered them all.

But then, standing before photos of preening men with glistening cleavage wearing boxers or bulging briefs, I thought of the twenty-year-old T-shirts and plain white underwear stacked in Ismail's dresser drawers. I recalled the cologne and shaving cream bottles lined up neatly below his sink—untouched presents from previous holidays—as well as the nearly identical shirts and sweaters hanging in his closet, all purchased on occasions like this. In a burst of inspiration, I knew what would mean the most to him: for me to turn around and leave this department store empty-handed, to defy Hallmark's insistence on this particular expression of love. So I went out on a limb and decided to give him the one present I never had before: nothing. Instead I'd found a piece of red construction paper among my daughter's art supplies, cut it into the shape of a heart, and scribbled reasons I loved him all over the back.

Later that night, after the dishes were done and Aliya's bath was finished, we set out in the dark for a nighttime walk. Leaving behind our warm, bright house that still smelled of the chicken we had roasted, we stepped into the bracing night air beneath a starlit canopy. We cut through our backyard and crossed into a meadow. A herd of deer lifted their heads in unison to stare at us, then froze like lawn ornaments as we passed by. We skirted the edge of the pond without speaking, our long strides falling into rhythm. On the far side of the meadow, we stepped onto the sidewalk and walked side by side. The damp pavement shimmered in the weak glow of a street lamp.

This was the time of day when we talked, when our thoughts meandered like these paths we followed through our neighborhood. His voice in my ear was a low purr, contented and pleasant. We walked briskly, our long shadows leading the way before us on the sidewalk. Ismail turned to me. "I'll never forget the gift you gave me today. Thank you."

I glanced at him, then back at our shadows bleeding together on the pavement. The Qur'an says that God is nearer to us than our own jugular vein, and there were moments when Ismail felt that close to me: nearer than my own skin, so close that I lost sight of him altogether. If I tried to describe that intimacy, each word was a wedge between us, cleaving us in two, creating concepts from a seamless whole. So I said nothing, focusing instead on the slender, faceless shadows before us. Merged together, they lumbered like one animal into the dark.

10 | *Welcome*

A crowd of relatives the size of a large tour group waited in the bright sunshine outside the Tripoli airport to welcome Ismail home for the first time in eight years. We had flown to Libya via New York and Milan so I could meet his family for the first time and we could introduce them to Aliya, then five years old. I was three months pregnant. Having trekked the Himalayas, camped along the Baja peninsula, and crossed Europe in trains, I considered myself a seasoned traveler. But if I'd known that the cappuccino I drank at the airport in Italy would be my last taste of coffee for the next three weeks, I would have felt more apprehensive about this trip. I was also unaware that the workout clothes neatly packed in my suitcase would remain untouched. None of my previous travels had prepared me for my arrival in Libya as the pregnant American wife of a firstborn Muslim son.

Ismail's youngest brother, Hussein, ran toward us and engulfed Ismail in a tight embrace, weeping and kissing his cheeks, while three of his sisters, in bright head scarves, circled around us. Like colorful, twittering birds that have found bird seed, they talked and laughed and pecked our cheeks, foreheads, and hands. They herded us into the parking lot and we crammed into tiny cars, counting each lap as an additional seat. The car I folded myself into with Aliya had no room for Ismail, so he ducked into a separate one. I found myself in a tiny hatchback with four adults and three small children who giggled and scrambled from lap to lap and from the front to the back of the car as we sped down a two-lane road through the desert.

We were headed to Ismail's family home, where he had been raised. Though we were probably traveling no more than forty miles per hour, it felt like we were going twice that speed in this tiny vehicle. I rested my elbow on a door that rattled on it hinges, and the floorboards beneath my feet strained and popped over the cracked and pothole-marked road. My husband's cousin, who was driving, spoke to me either in heavily accented English or in Arabic—I couldn't tell which over the mad hum of the car's engine. I nodded and smiled as my teeth rattled in their sockets. Cars dodging oncoming traffic sped past women wrapped in colorful cloth who walked serenely along the narrow dirt shoulder of the road.

Ismail's hometown on the outskirts of Tripoli was a labyrinth of tangled, unmarked alleys whose intersections were marked by towering piles of trash. My husband's cousin sped down narrow dirt roads, dodging trash and animals and parked cars, then came to a stop along a high stone wall. We had arrived at my in-laws' house, and there was no sign of my husband anywhere. The children tumbled from the car and ran through an iron gate into a dusty courtyard where patches of brown grass baked in the sun. In one corner, a lime tree with fruit like hard green stones cast a spindly web of shade in the dirt. Laughing and talking to one another excitedly, my Libyan relatives herded me toward the front door. I gripped Aliya's hand tightly in my own and stepped across the threshold of a squat blocklike cement structure into a large room with cold tile floors. Yet another crowd of relatives, twice as large as our greeting party, was seated in a circle on thin floor cushions. The men looked down when I entered the room, avoiding eye contact, but the children stared wide-eyed, and the women met my gaze with exuberant smiles. At the far end of the room, seated cross-legged on the floor, was a heavyset old woman. A worn and faded piece of cloth was wrapped several times around her body like a toga, and her head was wrapped in a flowery scarf. Her knees pushed up against the soft cloth and her large breasts rested heavily in her lap. A thin green line ran from the center of her bottom lip down her chin.

"A tattoo," Ismail explained to me later, "inked onto her face by an elder the week before her wedding."

This was my mother-in-law, Njaima, or Hajja, as everyone called her since she had returned from making her obligatory pilgrimage to Mecca many years before. Her eyes, creased with deep wrinkles, brimmed with tears, and she murmured softly and reached up toward me like an ancient child. Holding tight to my daughter's hand, I crossed the room and sat at her feet as everyone watched. "*Marhaba,*" she said, taking my hand. *Welcome.* She leaned forward and cradled my daughter's plump cheeks between large, calloused hands. Tears streamed down her face. "*Masha Allah,*" she murmured over and over again. "*Masha Allah!*" Literally translated as "God has willed it," the phrase was often used to express appreciation for children and to remember that all beauty and goodness came from God.

She turned to me, covering my slender hands with her broad, leathery ones, and began to speak. I could not understand a word of her Arabic, and there was still no sign of Ismail anywhere. I listened closely to the rise and fall of her voice punctuated by long pauses when her eyes searched mine for understanding. I watched the tears pool in her rheumy eyes and imagined what she was telling me. What I read in her eyes I could feel in my bones: how much she had missed her son, how welcome I was in her home, how she adored her granddaughter. I took deep breaths and tried to hold her gaze. Then she pulled back, grabbed me by my shoulders, and looked me up and down, appraising her lean blonde daughter-in-law in jeans and running shoes. She shook her head, furrowed her brow in concern and disapproval, and muttered the same Arabic words she would repeat to me over and over again on this trip: *Daifa, Daifa. Kuli, Kuli!* Too skinny, too skinny! Eat, Eat!

It felt like hours before Ismail appeared in the doorway to join us. Hajja's face creased in ecstasy at the sight of her son, and she cradled his face in her hands. My husband sobbed like a little boy, and tears flowed throughout the room. She patted his cheeks, then rose and pulled me by the hand into her kitchen, turning back once to wag her finger at Ismail and accuse him of starving his wife. She seemed deeply disturbed by my athletic build, the result of years of recreational running and careful eating. To her, it was a sign that something was terribly wrong. From that moment until the day I left, she plied me constantly with powdered nut cookies, bowls of rice, jerk meat, and strong sweet cups of tea. Only when my mouth was full did she seem to be at ease.

Taking my seat on the floor among the women, I looked around and knew immediately which ones were Ismail's sisters. They bore a strong resemblance to their brother: thick black eyebrows, brown eyes like dark chocolate medallions, plump cheeks and skin the color of coffee and cream. Fauziya, Aida, Nura . . . I studied their faces and tried to remember their names. One was missing: where was Ismail's fourth sister?

In the corner of the room, a woman hung back in the doorway to the kitchen, quietly witnessing our arrival as if eavesdropping on this family reunion. She stood only a few feet away but seemed much farther from this exuberant welcome party that surrounded me. Unlike the other women with their bright makeup and colorful clothes, her face was plain and pale, and she wore a simple black *abaya,* or floor-length robe, and a white head scarf as plain as a cloth napkin. She wore a guarded expression, smiling shyly when she caught my eye and then dropping her gaze immediately and disappearing into the kitchen as if she had been caught indulging in something forbidden. Ismail's family ignored her so completely that I assumed she must be a servant—but domestic help seemed incongruous in this small home with its barren walls and sparsely appointed rooms.

When we had all seated ourselves on the floor—men in one tight circle and women in another—the woman in black swept quietly into the room with a tray of cookies and tea, kneeling to serve each of us in turn. Family members helped themselves to her offerings without addressing her or acknowledging her presence—but when she knelt before Ismail, he reached for her and cradled her cheeks with such love that I knew they must be related. He tugged at her arm and appeared to be coaxing her to sit, but she resisted him and continued around the circle. When she disappeared into the kitchen, Ismail stood and followed her. Startled, the men glanced from his departing back to one another, as if alarmed by his strange behavior. A moment later Ismail returned from the kitchen holding her hand, pulling her toward me like a reluctant child, though as she got closer I could see that worry lines already creased her face.

"This is my sister Wajida," he told me, and she blushed as she took my hand. For the rest of the evening, I only caught glimpses of her as she came and went from the kitchen, clearing dishes and offering fresh cups of tea. When the men's conversation reached a fevered pitch and their laughter ricocheted off the empty walls, when the women fell back against pillows cupping their full round bellies in their hands, when the children flopped down onto floor pillows giggling, Wajida haunted the edge of the room as silent as a ghost.

Throughout my long first afternoon in Libya, a steady stream of relatives filed through the house to inspect Hajja's American daughter-in-law and granddaughter. Hajja led each guest to where I was seated, and they stood over me smiling and speaking in Arabic. I smiled as warmly as I could—an effort that became increasingly difficult as the hours wore on—and they settled onto the floor around me, nested in flowing layers of cloth, and carried on animated conversations that went on for hours. Laughing loudly and slapping her thigh, Hajja elbowed me as if I were in on the joke. I cocked my head and listened to the melody and rhythm of their Arabic, trying to glean whatever I could from these foreign sounds. It was like hearing the hum of a television through a closed door, never getting the specifics, only the general mood of the discussion: joyful, serious, sympathetic. All through that long afternoon, Hajja watched me with a probing, open gaze like an outstretched hand.

Finally, Hajja lowered herself to the ground and sat cross-legged before me. She gestured toward my head and said something to Ismail. "She says you would look beautiful with your head covered," he translated, flashing me an apologetic look. I nodded and smiled politely, and she nodded emphatically and brought her hands together beneath her chin, miming the act of tying a scarf. She raised her eyebrows invitingly like she was suggesting a game for us to play, then raised herself up off the floor and disappeared into a back room. She returned clutching a silken head scarf covered with Technicolor fruit: Day-Glo oranges, glossy red apples, an ornate vine of electric green leaves. She knelt before me and gently placed it over my head, sweeping stray hair from my forehead and tucking it beneath the cloth, then tied it snugly beneath my chin as if I were a porcelain doll. The other women in the room, each of whom I was related to in ways I did not comprehend, smiled and bobbed their covered heads approvingly. With my head swaddled in bright cloth and all eyes upon me, I felt ridiculous. Smiling apologetically and shaking my head, I pulled the scarf off and handed it back to her, feeling both indignant and for the first time self-conscious about the hair that fell across my face.

It seemed that I spent hours gazing down at the floor of Hajja's crowded home. Sunlight poured across the concrete, then faded. Darkness pressed against the window, and the shadows of women in the kitchen boiling yet more water for fresh tea began to seem like a delirious dream. Five hours had passed since our arrival, and I was exhausted. I had not had a moment to myself except in the bathroom—and then, squatting on the low toilet, I'd listened to my sisters-in-law in whispered conference outside the door. I longed for privacy, and I'd hoped to stay in Tripoli's big new hotel, where oil executives and tourists congregated. I wanted a steaming-hot bath, a countertop on which to spread my toiletries, an adjustable thermostat and a heater that hummed through the night, drowning out the honking of horns on the crowded streets below.

Finally I went to find Ismail. Standing in the doorway of a narrow windowless room where a circle of men sat appearing to have a heated debate, I gestured frantically for his attention.

"Can we go to a hotel?" I whispered when he met me in the doorway and bent his head to hear my request. Behind him, a room full of men watched us with curiosity; the circle of women behind me had grown silent and was studying us as well.

I did not realize how offensive this proposal would be to his family, but Ismail did. He sighed and looked at me long and hard, then turned to his family. I could tell by his apologetic tone that this situation called for the utmost diplomacy. His gentle suggestion that we retire to a hotel was met with a moment of shocked silence as relatives stared at one another and at us incredulously. Then the room erupted in protest. Men and women shook their heads and wagged their fingers, their expressions cycling rapidly from outrage to insult to pleading disbelief. They insisted we stay in the finest accommodations they could offer: the half-built home of my sister-in-law Fauziya and her husband, Adel. In the midst of the uproar, Ismail turned to me helplessly and raised his palms to the air. There was nothing he could do to stop this tidal wave of hospitality.

Blinking back tears of frustration, I climbed into the backseat of another tiny, rusty car, and we sped off down a winding alley while I groped in the dark for seat belts that did not exist. At their home, Adel and Fauziya led us down a gray concrete hallway to a small, unpainted bedroom with black plastic taped over each gaping window frame to keep out the wind. We slept in their bed while they curled up in a room nearby on floor mats. After seventeen hours of travel and eight more of socializing, I fell exhausted into the bed beside Ismail and with Aliya curled on a cot jammed between the bed and the wall.

Before falling asleep, I turned to him in the dark and asked him to tell me the story of Wajida. In a low whisper, he explained that after his three sisters had been married, the man Wajida loved had approached her father, but her father had driven the suitor away. Instead of getting married, Wajida became the one to care for her parents in their old age. She was their social security, their retirement plan, their domestic help, and their in-home nurse. When her brothers completed law school in Tripoli or left for the United States and Malaysia for graduate degrees, when her sisters got married and moved into apartments in downtown Tripoli or farms in the country and celebrated the births of their children, Wajida remained trapped in the rooms in which she had been raised, where her father's angry outbursts echoed through empty rooms and her mother's bitter silence hung like acrid smoke in the air. Her parents no longer spoke to one another, instead relying on Wajida to deliver curt messages between them. Instead of changing diapers, she massaged swollen feet and arthritic hands. Instead of continuing her education she was apprenticed to her own mother, learning the intricacies of housekeeping, martyrdom, and unbreakable faith.

After Ismail told me about Wajida, he rolled over and fell into a deep sleep, but I lay wide awake, unable to settle down, my heart racing like a child's after a ghost story. How could a family do this: sacrifice one innocent life for the benefit of the rest? Suddenly it seemed to me that everyone I had met earlier that day was complicit in Wajida's servitude: Ismail's gracious, sweet-smelling sisters; his gentle brothers who dropped their eyes in modesty instead of meeting my gaze; his mother who wept and kissed her son's hands as if he were a saint and she his devoted follower; his father, who returned from the mosque and sat straight-backed and serene in his long woolen tunic, as regal as the Buddha; and Ismail himself, who had lived in an American college dorm and gone to rock concerts, jogged down the street shirtless and gone out on countless dates, all the while knowing about his sister's confinement. And now I, too, was complicit in her oppression.

Eventually I drifted off to sleep, but in the middle of the night I awoke with a start to see a dark form reaching for Aliya in her cot while my husband snored softly by my side. My adrenaline surged before I realized it was my sister-in-law, who had heard my daughter cough and slipped into our bedroom to soothe her and give her God knows what medicine. On previous travels, exhausted by foreign languages and unfamiliar customs, I'd withdrawn to hotels and bars filled with other travelers, all of us ready to commiserate about home and toast our adventures. But there would be no respite from crowded, generous, broken, resilient Libya.

11 | *Hijabi Barbie*

Awakened at dawn by the call to prayer crackling over the fuzzy loudspeaker of a nearby mosque, I slipped out of bed while Ismail slept. I greeted my sister-in-law in the hallway with my morning breath, my bed head, and my frown lines. She handed me a tiny cup and saucer, the kind children use at tea parties, filled with a frothy concoction. None of my relatives drank coffee, but as a special treat for me, Fauziya had purchased a small, expensive canister of Nescafé powder. I tilted the cup to my mouth, nearly emptying it in one gulp. Among my hosts there was no coffee, no alcohol, no television or Internet, and as I quickly realized, no outdoor exercise, since I could not be on the streets without an escort and without my skin covered. In Libya I was cut off from all my addictions at once, cold turkey—and under the watchful eye of my female relatives who scrutinized my every expression and tried to anticipate every need.

After breakfast, seven of us piled into a car not much bigger than a golf cart and drove to the home of Ismail's beloved aunt Fatama, swerving on dirt roads past potholes deep enough to swallow a tire. A Libyan flag flapped in the wind, as green and plain as the apron of a Starbucks employee. In my mind's eye I saw a barista offering me three sizes that started tall and grew from there, saw myself cradling a paper cup filled with rich, dark brew. Folded onto Ismail's lap in the backseat, my head brushing the torn vinyl ceiling, I whispered into his ear: "Is there a Starbucks on the way?" He chuckled, low and sympathetic, and squeezed me tighter.

His aunt Fatama squatted in the dust among the chickens behind a high stone wall, waiting for us. A beaming round woman swaddled in a brightly colored cloth from head to toe, with a tattoo that matched my mother-in-law's, she greeted us with kisses, tears, and prayers, then disappeared into her darkened home. She returned a moment later with a plate of french fries dusted with salt. At 9 A.M. we sat in her courtyard, dipping them in ketchup and warming our faces in the weak morning sun as her cats threaded through our legs and her chickens pecked the dust.

An hour later, it was time to drive to the home of Ismail's childhood friend Mahmoud, where we had been invited for lunch. My limbs already heavy and my mind sluggish from jet lag, I leaned against Ismail in the backseat as we bounced down the road, our hatchback dodging chickens and a goat who looked up lazily, his breakfast of trash hanging from his mouth. Concealed behind a high stucco wall, Mahmoud's courtyard was beautifully landscaped, with a clean-swept brick pathway to an ornate front door. He stood in his doorway in pleated slacks and spit-polished shoes that appeared to have never set foot on a dusty Libyan street. I stepped from the car and, without thinking, swung my arms wide to hug him. With an expression of alarm he leapt deftly to one side, as if dodging a snake attack, leaving me grasping at the air. He would not shake my hand or even hold my gaze during the entire time I was in Libya.

An official in Muammar Gaddafi's regime, Mahmoud wore tailored suits and Italian leather shoes each time I saw him, even on weekends. A cloud of fear hung in the air around him like cheap cologne; friends and even his own family addressed him with downcast eyes and ingratiating smiles. I only saw him smile once, and he wiped the expression off his face so quickly that I thought I must have imagined it. Mostly he sat sullenly among the men, the lit cigarette between his fingers sending a thin question mark of smoke swirling above his head. One of the wealthiest men in Ismail's hometown, he had a shiny Volkswagen Jetta in his driveway and a comfortable home enclosed by a wrought-iron gate. In the United States his would have been a solidly middle-class home, but in this labyrinth of dirt alleys and trash-strewn roads, parched lime trees and dusty, wandering chickens, his residence was startlingly opulent.

Mahmoud's wife was heard and sensed but rarely seen: a swirl of black cloth, the sound of clanking pots, the smell of simmering curry drifting to us from the kitchen. I glimpsed her round face suspended in a tent of black, her kind eyes encircled in thick black kohl, her hands delivering a brass platter of glass teacups. The dining room table was elaborately set for two, though there were eight of us present; Mahmoud had assumed that my daughter and I would eat in the kitchen with his wife and children while the men convened in the formal dining room.

With a cajoling smile, Ismail said something to him in Arabic. Mahmoud responded in a clipped voice, and the two men began to negotiate. Mahmoud's tone told me he was increasingly annoyed with Ismail, who was clearly refusing to back down. Finally Mahmoud tossed his hands into the air and retreated into the kitchen. A moment later his wife emerged to set two more places at the table. "Don't worry: you will be eating with us," Ismail whispered into my ear. I was grateful and uneasy. I could not decide what would be more uncomfortable for me: eating in the kitchen with a woman and children whose language I did not speak or eating among the men where I was obviously unwelcome.

I sat between Ismail and Aliya at the dining table. Mahmoud sat across from us, smoothing his napkin and avoiding my gaze, appearing to be as rattled as if I had insisted on dining with him bare-breasted. He was tense with the effort to deny my presence. Every now and then his eyes darted toward me, but he yanked them away like dogs on a short leash. Mostly I kept my eyes on my plate, raising them only to thank Mahmoud's wife guiltily and effusively each time she emerged from the kitchen to serve me another dish.

After dinner we moved to another room to lounge on floor pillows, and Mahmoud's wife and children joined us there. The floor pillows at Ismail's mother's house were only inches thick, but the ones at Mahmoud's were plush and ornately embroidered with gold thread. We relaxed into them and Mahmoud placed a gift in Aliya's lap: a Muslim Barbie doll covered from her neck to her toes in a black abaya. Just a few wisps of her brassy blonde hair slipped out from beneath her head scarf, but the face that stared up at Aliya was as familiar as an old friend from home: wide, sky blue eyes; slightly parted bubble gum lips; a brilliant white smear of teeth.

Something besides her clothing was fundamentally different about her; something essential was missing. It took me a few moments to realize what it was: her torpedo breasts, those un-yielding nipple-free mounds. Her chest was as flat as if she had gotten a double mastectomy.

The Barbie stared up at Aliya with her impenetrable smile.

The room fell silent as we waited for Aliya's reaction. I silently willed her to show gratitude and delight, but instead she stared down at the doll with a furrowed brow, her lips pursed in concentration. This Barbie was a riddle she couldn't solve.

After a few moments of befuddled contemplation, her face lit up with an idea. She yanked the head scarf from the doll's head, freeing the brassy blonde hair, which she combed with her chubby fingers until it lay down her back. The narrow strip of cloth she smoothed out onto the carpet beside her, considering it carefully. Next she yanked the abaya wide open, its Velcro strips resisting before giving way to her insistent fingers, revealing Barbi's peach-colored near nudity in plain white granny underwear and what looked like a Jogbra. Now I could see that her figure was childlike: gone, too, were her pencil-thin waist and voluptuous hips. Aliya tugged at the undergarments, but they were sewn to the doll's flesh, not to be removed under any circumstances.

All eyes in the room rested on the disrobed doll splayed out on the floor. The dolls at our house were shameless, always in a state of partial undress. When I found them lounging topless on our furniture or lying spread-eagle in an empty bathtub, I stepped over them without giving them a second thought. But in this foreign world, her exposed peachy flesh made me squirm. I had to resist the urge to cover her up. Aliya cocked her head like Versace considering a half-dressed model. Then, in a burst of inspiration, she grabbed the strip

of cloth that had once been a head scarf and was now a ban-
dera. She cinched it tightly around the doll's bottom, turning
it into the smallest miniskirt imaginable and tying it rakishly
at the hip. Her eyes lit up with pleasure and pride; now the
doll was ready to play.

12 | *Freedom*

Hussein had been the first to embrace us when we arrived in Libya. He was over six feet tall and thirty years old, the first slivers of gray hair already streaking his temples, but he had raced down the sidewalk outside the Tripoli airport and clung to his big brother like a little boy, wiping tears from his cheeks with the back of his hand. Next he'd turned to Aliya, lifting her gently from my arms and kissing her on each chubby cheek. His display of vulnerability and raw emotion evoked a tenderness I usually only feel toward small children. From the first moment I saw him, he was our quiet and gentle companion in Libya, often hovering in the background, his hand appearing before me just in time to open a door, refill a cup of tea, or sweep Aliya from the sidewalk before she stepped in a puddle.

The other men in Ismail's family refused to meet my gaze for more than a few seconds, staring instead down at my knees when we were introduced, but Hussein let his curious eyes linger on mine before dropping them again toward the floor.

When our eyes met, he could not suppress a shy, boyish smile. Like the sun momentarily appearing between the clouds, his smile lit up his whole face before it was concealed once again behind an impassive masculine front. Like Ismail, he seemed more at home with his laughing, affectionate sisters than with the men, who spoke over him and addressed him in clipped tones. He responded by springing from the floor to do whatever had been asked of him.

Having graduated from college seven years prior, Hussein was still living at home with his parents and biding his time until the government, Libya's main employer, placed him in a job. Seven years was not an unusually long time to wait. He seemed frozen in time, trapped in a prolonged adolescence even as his hair began to recede and his belly began to spill over his pants. He inhabited the same small rooms where he had been raised, slept on the same floor cushions on which he had lain as a child, his long legs and large feet now spilling onto the floor. He had spent all of his twenties under the brooding, critical eye of his father and within arm's reach of his doting mother. When he first approached us, I had seen a full-grown man, handsome and broad-shouldered, walking down the sidewalk with a purposeful stride. But when he bent his head and ducked through the doorway of his family home, he seemed to shrink in age and stature, to become once again the baby boy of the family: subservient to his father and older brothers, affectionate and attentive toward his mother and his sisters.

One day, when I was seated alone on the floor, Hussein sat down only inches away, closer than any man but Ismail had been to me since I had arrived in Libya. He pulled a worn leather wallet from his pocket and dug into it to find a postage stamp–sized snapshot. Blushing, he pressed it surreptitiously into my hand. I held it up to my face to study the plain, serious face of a young woman in a dark head covering. She stared into the camera as if posing for a mug shot. The snapshot was creased and yellow at the edges; it must have been tucked away in his wallet for years.

"My fiancée," Hussein said proudly, in halting English.

Ismail had never mentioned anything to me about the fact that Hussein had a girlfriend, much less that he was engaged. For a moment I felt a bitter righteousness; I had often complained to him about his failure to share important information about his family, details I needed in order to be a gracious daughter- or sister-in-law.

I held the photo up close and studied the woman's face more carefully, this time seeing her through Hussein's eyes: arched black eyebrows as precise as calligraphy strokes, full lips, round cheeks, and flawless skin. "She's beautiful," I murmured, handing the photo back to him.

Hussein nodded and flashed me a quick smile like we were in on a secret, then slipped the photo back into his wallet like money he was saving for the future. He told me his fiancée had sat on the opposite side of the room in his accounting class at the university. They had exchanged smiles over the heads of other students and had spoken a few words in the hallway or walking the pathways across campus. In one of those stolen moments, he had fallen in love. Like tumbling from a high place, like gravity's swift and inexorable pull, it took no time at all for him to realize he wanted to spend the rest of his life with her. He had asked her parents for her hand in marriage, and the day they consented, seven years ago, she had given him the photo that he had just shared with me.

I imagined this young woman in her early twenties, celebrating her engagement—and then waiting under her parents' roof, just like he had been doing, for seven long years. After all this time, had he become as difficult to recall as the math formulas she had learned in that class? Was she still as excited about her engagement now that her thirties loomed and the first fine crow's-feet were appearing around the edges of her eyes?

"When do you see her?"

Sometimes driving down the streets of his hometown, he caught a glimpse of her walking with her mother or her sister: a flash of full cheek, the swivel of a round hip beneath flowing cloth. Sometimes in the market he saw her slender fingers reaching for fresh fruit or heard her distinct laughter floating above the chatter of vendors and shoppers.

"When is your wedding?"

He shook his head and furrowed his brow. Not until he had finished building his own house on the small plot of land beside his parents' home, he said, pointing toward the barren courtyard. He would pay for the construction himself, with wages earned at his long-anticipated government job; he and his family would lay the foundation and build it piece by piece as he could afford to purchase the materials. In other words, it seemed as if he might be no more than halfway through his engagement. He would be lucky to wed before his bride's eggs began to wither.

It seemed to me that nearly every person I encountered in Libya was waiting for something: a job, a house, a visa, a spouse, a car, a future. A lone shopkeeper in the market sat on an overturned crate, waiting with a faraway look in his eyes for customers who never arrived. Young men loitered on street corners all hours of the day, hands thrust deep into jeans pockets, scanning passing traffic as if impatiently waiting to flag down their futures like taxis. My sister-in-law, at home all day with two small children—without a car, sidewalks on which to push a stroller, or a park nearby where they could play—sat in her kitchen and stared out the window, clutching a cup of tea already cold in her palms, waiting for her husband's return while her children's shrieks bounced off the barren walls.

An impenetrable bureaucracy was cast like a fishing net over the entire country, trapping Libyans in place; the more they thrashed against their constraints, the more they engaged the dysfunctional system, the more tangled and paralyzed they became. The moment I had stepped onto Libyan soil, I felt the weight of this net falling over me. When the plane taxied to the gate at the Tripoli airport, I leapt from my seat and reached into the overhead bin, eager to be one of the first to enter the airport. If I had been paying attention, I might have noticed how slowly other passengers were now moving; this would have given me a clue of what was to come. One of the first to enter the airport, I immediately found myself in a stock-still line that snaked out the door. The line surged forward when a man at a desk waved an entire group through without even looking at their paperwork.

Then it came grinding to a halt. Up ahead at customs, a middle-aged man sat at a desk, now and then calling to a tight cluster of men who huddled in the corner in a nicotine cloud, eyeing those of us who had just arrived with hostile suspicion. For the next hour, we stood in place or stepped forward inches at a time, scanning the plain, stained walls for something to hold our interest, finding only Gaddafi's massive portrait to contemplate. The men who appeared to be in charge took long drags off their cigarettes and carried on animated conversations in Arabic, like old friends who had gathered here to share news and gossip. They seemed oblivious to the line of exhausted, impatient travelers that spilled beyond this room. This was a perfect initiation to life in Tripoli.

In Ismail's mother's home, my waiting began in earnest. I waited to be told where to sit, then for tea to be served. I waited to go to the bathroom; to talk to Ismail, who was engrossed in conversation with the men in another room; to go for a walk, since my family insisted I needed a chaperone. I waited to be driven downtown, and when we had finally gotten to the old city market and Gaddafi announced without warning that all stores must immediately close so he could make a speech on television, I returned home and waited for his announcement that stores could reopen. (That announcement came days later.)

I belonged to a world where, with one mouse click, I could purchase a plane ticket, track down an old boyfriend, chat with childhood friends now living in California, China, or Ethiopia. I could order a meal to be delivered to my door in minutes; jump in my car and head to the mall, grocery store, or cafe to satisfy any craving; lace up my running shoes and disappear into the woods. Thanks to such dizzying freedom, I had friends all over the world. I was well traveled, well dressed, and physically strong—and very, very bad at waiting. Especially when it came to my addictions.

My first few days in Libya, each time I saw a flash of Gaddafi's signature green in the distance, I imagined, like a mirage, a green Starbucks goddess beckoning to me from a distant storefront. My heart sank when I realized it was a figment of my imagination, but an equally appealing sign made my heart race when we pulled up to the curb beside it: a small, hand-painted sign that read INTERNET. Hussein worked part-time there, in a dim, narrow room lined with dated computers. We ducked inside. Hussein sat at the front desk and I sat down at a terminal beside a teenager watching a YouTube video, her earplugs tucked beneath her head scarf. The sight of Google popping up on my screen was as familiar and comforting as the sight of my own front door. I would have been happy to sit there all day long checking news headlines, scanning the weather, emailing friends. Even checking work email felt like a vacation.

Suddenly two skinny boys in matching green fatigues burst through the front door yelling in Arabic. Their voices ricocheted off the empty walls, and the rifles slung over their shoulders swung like toys against their hips. Startled teenagers in tunics or *hijabs* looked up, then froze like statues and locked their gazes on the screens before them. Hussein curled his shoulders inward and dropped his eyes to the ground. The boys, who appeared to be half his age, squared their skinny chests and barked orders, raising their voices over one another as if in contest to see who could be the loudest. They would have seemed comical if not for the fear that blew through the room like a cold wind.

Hussein nodded and murmured placating sounds, and then they turned abruptly and left, slamming the door behind them and peeling away from the curb in a shiny new German car. When I asked Hussein what their visit had been about, he told me they were from Gaddafi's internal security force and that they had come to demand that he take down the small storefront's Internet sign. Gaddafi had banned the English alphabet from Libyan streets. I looked out at the small, sun-faded sign, its paint peeling at the edges. How long had it been hanging there? About three years, Hussein said, the left side of his mouth lifting into an ironic smile. I looked longingly back at the computer monitor before me. I wanted to climb inside the screen, hook myself to the Internet with an IV, numb myself from the unrelenting strangeness of this country. But Hussein rose from his seat and gestured toward the car. It was time to go; my sister-in-law Fauziya was expecting me.

FAUZIYA WAS A tall, slender woman with sculpted black eyebrows and a porcelain complexion. She commanded respect both inside and outside the home. It was evident in her quiet authority over her children, in the attentive way her husband listened to her, in the way shopkeepers in the market brightened at the sight of her and hurried to meet her requests. Before she left her house she applied red lipstick, slipped on high-heeled Italian boots, and wrapped a scarf expertly around her head so that it hugged her face and fell in silken ripples over her neck. When she returned home, she slipped off her boots and removed her head scarf in the foyer, shaking loose a thick black mane that fell down her back. To my eye, the black curls that framed and softened her face transformed her swiftly from foreign to familiar.

At her half-built home in an arid field there were no sidewalks, no walking paths, no nearby parks where the children could play. One day Ismail left me there while he tried to track down his passport, which had been confiscated from us at customs. (Ten days before, when we had arrived, an airport official had tucked it into the pocket of his cheap polyester workshirt, waving us on with a promise to return it to us sometime in the next few days. We had heard nothing since.) I sat in her drafty house, where children delirious with boredom tore from room to room with high-pitched squeals. When I couldn't bear the sound any longer I moved to the front steps, where I squatted and tilted my face toward the weak morning sun.

I was increasingly desperate to escape Fauziya's excruciating patience and grace. She seemed unphased by the cold wind pawing at the black plastic, the shrieks of the children, the watery Nescafé she served. She smiled warmly at me as she washed yet another stack of dishes, and I tried to prevent my restlessness from exploding into full-blown rage: Where was Ismail? When would I finally get a few minutes to myself? Where could I get a real cup of coffee? And what kind of a goddamn vacation was this, anyway? My swollen American ego was a serious liability in this country—a heavy burden like an unwieldy, overstuffed bag I hauled everywhere, often enduring incriminating glances from in-laws who had never before seen a woman weighed down by so much individualism, impatience, and desire. Libya's rough terrain was far too treacherous for me to be hauling around this much baggage. Fauziya's ego, like a lightweight backpack containing only the barest essentials, was far more suitable; patience and humility cultivated over a lifetime allowed her to gracefully scale Libya's formidable obstacles and navigate its tight spaces.

One morning, with another long day stretching out before us and very little to do, I sat on the edge of Fauziya's bed, watching her prepare for a trip to the grocery store. I asked her to show me how she wrapped her head scarf so that it fit so snugly around her face and fell so elegantly to her shoulders. She selected a rectangular brown cloth from her closet, soft as a cotton jersey, then stood before me and tented it over my head, carefully lining up the edges. She swept it twice around my face and tucked it neatly beneath my chin with a pin. I hurried to the bathroom to examine myself in the mirror. With my hair no longer exposed, my blue eyes and long face seemed somehow even more so. The scarf hugged my face, warm and snug. It did not feel smothering, as I had assumed it would. Instead it offered privacy, warmth, and protection. I was startled by how different I looked—and how comfortable I felt.

The next time I joined Fauziya on a shopping trip downtown, I followed the steps she had shown me to wrap the scarf around my own head. I felt self-conscious when I stepped into the living room wearing it for the first time, but only Aliya stared wide-eyed and openmouthed from where she stood in the doorway. My in-laws smiled and complimented me. On Libyan streets the scarf was a reassuring barrier, protecting me from chilly coastal breezes and the curious stares of strangers.

One morning not long after, Aliya emerged from her bedroom with her white cotton tights pulled snugly down around her head, concealing all her hair. Flaccid leggings fell on either side of her face. Her four-year-old cousin stood by her side, his arm locked in hers, his own head swaddled in a towel. They explained to us they were aunties visiting for tea, so we offered them tiny cups filled with warm milk. While we stood in the kitchen, they sat at our feet sipping from them. Fauziya leaned forward and reached for my hand, as if she was about to break some difficult news. She wore a floor-length housedress and her thick black hair was swept into a high twist off her neck. Her gold earrings swayed like pendulums as she leaned in toward me.

"Sometimes you make me nervous," she said, arching one perfectly shaped eyebrow.

I froze, both taken aback and intrigued by her candor. "Why?"

Her hands fluttered in the air as she reached for just the right English words to diplomatically express what she needed to say. Finally, lacking the vocabulary to soften her statement, she threw her hands into the air.

"You don't act like a woman."

In sweatpants and one of Ismail's old running T-shirts, I leaned back against her kitchen counter, speechless. I had just fit a baseball cap onto my head and was about to lace up my running shoes. My plan was to jog a few brisk laps around the crabgrass field behind her home to get my aerobic exercise before spending the rest of the day indoors among the women.

Seeing my shocked expression, Fauziya rushed to explain. "You insist on doing everything yourself: always carrying your own bags, always making your own plans, always going, going, going. How can your husband treat you like a woman if you don't act like one?"

Her comment struck me in a sensitive place. Back home, when Muslim friends hosted large mealtime gatherings, I was always offered a seat smack in the middle of a long table, the women to my left and the men to my right—a border zone I jokingly referred to in private with Ismail as the transgendered seating area. My seating assignment confirmed that others recognized what I felt in the company of our Muslim friends: I didn't quite belong with the men *or* the women. I was most comfortable in the margins between the women's gentle laughter and quiet intimacies and the men's long-winded political or religious debates. Now I could see that my sister-in-law recognized a similar quality in me. But what had I done to call my femininity into question? Then I remembered when we had first arrived at her house, as I struggled to maneuver my heavy suitcase up the front stairs in the dark, her husband, Adel, had backed up the stairs before me one by one with an outstretched hand, pleading with me to let him carry my bag.

In my exhaustion I had waved him off and plowed forward, focused only on finding the shortest path to bed. My shins were still bruised where the suitcase had banged against them.

"You're pregnant," Fauziya said to me now, slowly and clearly. She held my gaze and searched my eyes for understanding. "You should put your feet up and rest. This is the time for your husband to serve you—but how can he do that if you never lie down?"

I crossed my arms over my chest, feeling defensive and unsettled by her words. This pregnancy had brought on exhaustion like a leaden weight I dragged with me everywhere. The only way I knew how to deal with fatigue like this was to bend into it and press forward; I feared that if I stopped for even a moment, it might swallow me whole. With a full-time job, a young daughter, a marriage, a fitness routine, and an active social life to maintain, I couldn't afford to be sidelined. Even when Ismail had suggested this trip to Libya during my first trimester, I had not paused to consider how difficult it would be to make such a long journey while I was so nauseated and tired. Pregnancy, as I understood it, was no excuse for laziness. At my last prenatal visit, my doctor and I had brainstormed ways to combat my enervation—with a cup of coffee in the morning, a good diet, regular exercise. There was no reason I couldn't continue running through my second trimester, she said. Perhaps I should also consider prenatal yoga for relaxation and stress relief; I seemed a little tense.

So I had signed up for a local prenatal yoga class. Once a week I left work just before 5 P.M. and drove to a nearby studio, a backpack of workout clothes slung over my shoulder and a rolled yoga mat beneath my arm. Expectant mothers in yoga gear unfolded from minivans and station wagons and convened in a room with gleaming hardwood floors and a wall of windows. We sat in a circle on colorful mats, our bottles of filtered water beside us. Our instructor, heavily pregnant with her second child, sat before us like a spandex-clad fertility goddess, her back ramrod straight, her skin glowing and flushed like she'd just stepped from a sauna. She was a feast of feminine curves: breasts the size of cantaloupes spilling from a tank top like a second skin, a watermelon belly she cradled with freshly manicured hands, buttocks so high and round it was as if she had breast implants in her rear end.

The first night of class, she asked us to introduce ourselves one by one around the circle. Several women offered their own names and then, patting their swollen bellies, proudly added, *This is Lily. This is Jackson. This is Olivia.* The rest of us nodded and smiled as if genuinely pleased to make these tiny new fetal acquaintances. Caressing her belly, the instructor encouraged us in a singsong voice to close our eyes and *connect* with our babies, to *invite* them into the world and to let them know how *welcome* they were. I stole glances at women smiling blissfully with eyes closed, rubbing their midsections in gentle circles like the Buddha's belly. I chewed the inside of my cheek. I checked my watch. Beneath my old cotton T-shirt, my midsection was thick like a tire, not round like a moon, and I had no idea how to be a gracious host to my womb's tiny guest, which I only knew by the names *exhaustion, indigestion,* and *bloating.* The class had not even begun, and already it was beginning to feel more stressful than my day at the office.

I quickly discovered that prenatal yoga was not about relaxing, exactly: it was about relaxing *into pain.* This was a critical distinction. As we contorted and panted and the blood rushed to our faces, our instructor encouraged us to notice our breath and befriend the burn in our muscles. The only moment of stillness came at the very end of class, when the instructor dimmed the lights and turned up the sound track of waves breaking onto shore, and for five minutes we curled up on our sides in a modified child's pose. My heavy, tired body melted into the floor. I closed my eyes, grateful for my first restful pause in twelve hours. I craved silence as much as stillness, but over the sound of breaking waves, the instructor began to tell us about her experience of childbirth. Over the course of the entire six-week class she never ran out of instructive anecdotes from her moment of bloody glory. We learned about the doula who baked cookies and eased her in and out of the tub, the husband who burned incense and massaged her lower back, the professional photographer who dimmed the lights and caught it all on film. Among these women, pregnancy felt like a competitive feat of endurance and style, a proving ground for our womanhood and our marriages.

I thought my job was not to surrender to pregnancy; instead I forced my pregnancy to submit to my busy life. But the moment Fauziya suggested lying down, I realized that was what I most wanted permission to do. With every inch of my being, I ached for rest. I wanted to curl up on her soft bedspread in the middle of the day with a cup of tea and a book, to stare out the window and contemplate the crabgrass field or doze back into the pillows. I wanted to stop mincing time like an onion into tiny, symmetrical units; I wanted the hours to ooze and puddle like syrup, sweet and slow. I wanted my to-do list to evaporate like steam from a kettle. For just one day I wanted to curl up on the couch and watch the soap opera of the improbable arc of the sun: the joy of its brilliant rise, the mournfulness of its fall. And I wanted to eat, *really* eat, not what was most nutritious but what pleased me most, to relish flavors and fullness and then to stretch out, sleepy and satisfied. Perhaps in Libya, stranded among family for days with nothing to accomplish and nowhere to go, I could finally do just that.

Fauziya wanted to know what I planned to do when the baby arrived. I proudly explained to her that my plan was to negotiate a longer maternity leave than anyone at my office had ever secured: eight whole weeks at home with my newborn. Knowing that I would be pushing the limits with my request for so much time, I would build my case methodically. I'd determine my dollar value to my employer, tally my financial contributions to the organization over the past four years in an Excel spreadsheet. I'd lay out plans to avoid taking time off all year so I could use my paid vacation days when the baby came. I'd emphasize that immediately after the baby was born I would make myself available by phone or email for any urgent needs during my absence.

Fauziya listened closely. And who would care for my baby when I returned to work? she wanted to know. I was not yet sure. I had already been investigating local day-care providers and was particularly interested in one that had very good ratios—only four babies per caregiver—but could barely afford it on my current salary.

Why not just quit work? she asked.

I shook my head. That was simply not an option—not with our debt and mortgage and the high cost of college education. Plus Ismail's job always seemed uncertain; he worked for a corporation that laid off staff even in years when the company turned extraordinary profits. It had simply become too difficult for an American family to enjoy a middle-class life on just one income.

"Besides," I added a bit too quickly and defensively, seeing her doubtful look, "I like working. Earning my own money gives me freedom." Fauziya cocked her head slightly, and I could have sworn I saw pity flash across her face.

Later that week, at a museum of Roman artifacts where a

gleaming marble bust of Gaddafi was shamelessly on display beside an ancient and chipped one of a Roman emperor, Ismail purchased me a copy of *The Green Book,* Gaddafi's rambling political manifesto, which was mandatory reading for all Libyans, the number-one best-selling book in the country for decades. On our drive home I thumbed through the book, reading aloud Gaddafi's "solution to the problem of democracy." Proclamations like "Labour for wages is the same as enslaving human beings" or "Popular rule does not mean popular expression" reminded me of the epiphanies that coalesced in the thick marijuana haze of a college dorm room: seemingly brilliant to an addled mind, utterly incomprehensible in the sober light of day. I did my best Gaddafi imitation, and Ismail laughed and shook his head, keeping his eyes on the road.

Scanning Gaddafi's manifesto for more outrageous quotes to read aloud, I fell silent when I read these words: "To demand equality in carrying heavy weights while the woman is pregnant is unjust and cruel . . . as is demanding equality in hardship while she is breastfeeding." The words tugged at a knot deep in my chest; something in me began to unravel. The text blurred as tears sprang to my eyes. I had not expected to discover plain truth here, in the unhinged proclamations of a mad dictator; I did not expect to find myself in grateful agreement with this tyrant.

Ismail glanced over at me, startled to see my expression turn from silly to serious. Everywhere I turned back home, I saw advertisements for products and services that promised to help me juggle work and family, to make me sexy and successful and make motherhood easy—as if serenity could be bought in installments as long as cash flowed as steadily as the milk from my breasts. In nine months I would be sitting in the only secluded space in my workplace: perched on the toilet in the cramped employee bathroom, pumping milk from sore and swollen breasts to freeze for my newborn, who would spend his days with a stranger on the other side of town. At least Libyans knew the face of their tyranny: his bulbous nose, his flamboyant style, his vacant stare. Fear permeated my life as well, forced me to yield what was most precious to me, strangled my sense of possibility. And I didn't even know where it came from.

13 | *Rage*

Adel and Fauziya wrestled the bucket seats of their rusty hatchback forward so Ismail and I could fold ourselves into the back, knees to chest, on a bench seat with foam padding bursting from torn vinyl seams. We were on our way to the desert mountain village where my brother-in-law's Berber family lived. There were no seat belts and none of the three young children in the car—my daughter, my niece, and my nephew—had seats anyway. Instead they clambered from lap to lap as we drove: small bodies tumbling from the back to the front, tiny hands grasping the steering wheel for balance, feet teetering across the emergency brake as if it were a balancing beam, cheeks pressing up against each dusty window. It was like taking a road trip with three feral cats.

For two hours, we drove on a two-lane road that cut through an endless arid landscape and then climbed a steep mountain pass. We had to shout to hear one another over the whining of the children and the car's overtaxed engine, which buzzed like a fat, low-flying mosquito in our ears and rattled the car's tinny doors and floorboards. In a tiny cluster of homes in the middle of nowhere, my brother-in-law swerved off the road and parked in a ditch beside a house built into the side of a mountain.

A round-faced woman with a bright smile welcomed us at the door, a small child clutching at her skirt and peeking out from behind her broad hips. Somewhere behind her, animated voices bounced off bare walls. She led us down a dark hallway to a narrow, crowded room with only one high window on its far side. Beneath the window, seated on a floor cushion as if it were a throne, sat the family patriarch, holding court over a circle of men. A separate, noisier circle of women and children filled the other half of the room. The only piece of furniture was a seventies-era television with rabbit ear antennae that towered over us on a wooden stand, its volume turned all the way down.

When I turned to find my seat among the women, I saw that the room contained one more piece of furniture: flush against the back wall was a narrow metal hospital bed on rusty wheels. A white sheet concealed the bony outline of a skeletal figure. Her wizened face stared unblinking toward the ceiling: sunken cheeks, gaping mouth, unseeing eyes as pale and washed out as the blue-white desert sky. She looked like a corpse—but then air wheezed from her lungs with a high-pitched whine that sounded like a leaky balloon. This was my brother-in-law's dying grandmother.

Never in my life had I seen anyone this close to death—and certainly not in a bed placed like a buffet table along the wall of a crowded party. This woman looked like she belonged in an intensive care unit, under twenty-four-hour supervision by medical staff, with machines to monitor each labored breath and frail heartbeat. Images from our long drive through the desert flashed through my mind: nothing for miles but dust and sky, olive trees and cliff faces, the occasional passing car. What could possibly be done for her in such a remote area, in this barren home that lacked good lighting or even a decent chair, that seemed to lack everything but family and food?

I was clearly the only one alarmed by her condition; everyone else was totally relaxed in her presence, chatting with her or maneuvering around her bed. Dying was apparently as much a part of a busy Libyan household as all the other chaos of family: the eating and drinking and playing and reprimanding now taking place in this small room. My brother-in-law went straight to his grandmother and kissed her head. Next Ismail approached the bed. He covered her bony fingers with his hand, knelt down, and kissed her forehead and spoke to her. He pulled me toward him and gestured silently that I should greet her, so I mumbled something self-consciously to her in English, feeling awkward and trying to avoid staring at those milky eyes.

I was offered a seat on the floor almost directly beneath the hospital bed—if I leaned back, its metal leg prodded me in the back, reminding me not to get too comfortable. A huge silver platter with the circumference of a truck tire was placed at the center of the circle: dinner was served. On either side of me women leaned forward and reached into a mountain of fragrant rice and chicken parts, dipping their slender fingers into an oily yellow sauce. The rattling breaths of the dying grandmother mingled in the air with the chatter of women and the giggles of children. A baby wriggled free from its mother's lap and crawled under the hospital bed, grasping its rickety metal frame and trying to stand on fat legs. As she always did at gatherings like these, my sister-in-law Fauziya sat by my side, eating and gesturing animatedly, throwing her head back and laughing without ever losing contact with my body—her warm thigh against mine, her hand resting for a moment on my leg, her fingers squeezing my arm, guiding me gently through this daunting afternoon as if maneuvering a blind person through heavy traffic.

Because I could not join the conversation, I began to focus instead on the silent images scrolling across the grainy television screen on the opposite side of the room. Pale-faced soldiers in bulky camouflage, weighed down with ammunition, were herding together dark skinny boys and men. In their heavy black boots, the soldiers swaggered and stomped, gesturing with guns toward captives who knelt in the dust. The crouched men stared up at the steely faces of soldiers whose eyes were concealed behind mirrored sunglasses that appeared to block out suffering along with UV rays.

Suddenly, close-up shots of bloody, broken brown bodies began to scroll across the screen—images I had never seen on American television. Back home, war was a televised spectacle of the latest military technology: tanks rolling single file down abandoned roads, jets lifting off from aircraft carriers, rockets sizzling like fireworks through a nighttime sky. War was young men returning home as heroes to ecstatic, beautiful wives; kneeling, arms open to embrace clean, delighted children. On Libyan television war was a dirty affair—grittier than a reality TV show, bloodier than an R-rated action flick. Brown faces young and old, naked with rage, teemed in a rundown street. The camera panned in on a child's corpse lying in the dust beside a puddle of blood black as oil. A woman covered in cloth wept and wailed over the tiny body, her face naked with grief.

I glanced nervously around me. Thankfully, I seemed to be the only one watching television. What must people who saw images like these on a regular basis think about me when I flew halfway around the world for a short vacation in the country they had never been allowed to leave, when I sat impatiently among them in my jeans and tennis shoes? When they opened their doors to me, did it occur to them how much I resembled these soldiers on television? Why did they continue day after day to offer me the very best of what they had, to kiss my cheeks and cuddle my child and smile at me from across the room with such love and acceptance?

Raising his voice to be heard over the din, the patriarch turned and addressed Ismail. He gestured grandly toward me with one hand, and his voice rose with a question. The room fell silent as the guests turned first to me, then back to Ismail to await his response. I shot a quizzical look at Fauziya, who leaned over and whispered, "He just asked Ismail what his American wife thinks of our country." Like everyone else, I turned my face expectantly toward my husband to await his response.

Ismail shook his head slowly from side to side and screwed up his face into an expression of disgust, as if he'd just tasted something foul that he needed to spit into a napkin. When he began to speak, Fauziya's hand tightened involuntarily around my arm, and she let out a little gasp. The bright smiles in the room flattened into tight lines and pursed lips. I could feel my husband's betrayal in my bones.

"What's he saying?" I whispered to Fauziya. She was hanging on his words, her mouth shaped into an *O* of surprise. She shook her head quickly back and forth, as if trying to jolt herself from a bad dream. When I repeated my question, she turned to me hesitantly and bit her lip. I could tell she was torn between her sisterly allegiance to me, which demanded she tell me the truth, and her reluctance to translate out of a desire to protect me. "He says you hate it here," she whispered curtly, offering only a brief summary of what Ismail was still taking his time to elaborate upon in great detail with a theatrical voice and animated hand gestures.

I watched his eyebrows rise and fall, his lips curl into a frown, his tea-stained teeth flash between his thick lips. I watched him pause to lick chicken grease from his fingers, then crack a joke that made the rest of the men snort and chuckle and steal glances in my direction, their round bellies jiggling beneath their tunics. I trained my eyes on his face so that when he caught my gaze he could see he was lined up squarely in the crosshairs of my fury. When our eyes met, he jerked his gaze away like yanking his hand from an open flame.

My rage was a loaded gun I held close to my chest for the rest of the afternoon in this crowded room. As the women around me socialized, I sat alone with my resentment, fantasizing about my first opportunity to pull the trigger. That moment would not come for several hours, not until we left this crowded room, not until I had escaped this suffocating circle of women who seemed to only be at peace when my mouth was full of food. Oblivious to my anger, they plied me with plate after plate of chicken, followed by syrupy-sweet green tea and buttery pastries. I gnawed on my anger as I stuffed my queasy stomach. Safely enclosed in the circle of men, Ismail was avoiding eye contact with me altogether. Somewhere between the crowded house and the overfull car, I imagined, in my first private moment with him, I would launch my retaliation.

By the time we finally escaped that room, I could barely contain myself. But the entire herd of our extended relatives, everyone except the dying woman, poured out into the street, circling around while we folded like circus clowns back into the tiny car. As soon as the engine revved up and we pulled away from all those faces pressed against each dusty window, I exploded.

"What the hell were you thinking?" I sputtered in Ismail's ear as the mosquito engine whined to life and the children began to squirm and crawl.

"I was just telling the truth!" he shot back—both of us pretending our angry whispers could not be heard by my in-laws inches away or the children scrambling over our laps. "All I've heard from you since we've gotten here is how much you hate this place!"

This was an exaggeration and a low blow, but I could not deny that I had cursed his native country. When we'd passed through airport customs and the sullen official had tucked Ismail's passport into the pocket of his workshirt, he'd mumbled to Ismail that the passport would be returned in a few days' time via the cousin of a brother of the husband of a neighbor. Somehow, even though we weren't even yet sure where we would be staying, he was confident that he would be able to find us. *"Mish mishkla,"* he'd said, shrugging and waving us through the line. *No problem.* It was the most popular phrase in the Libyan vocabulary, I quickly discovered, one I heard many times a day—always with a cavalier shrug of the shoulders or a wave of the hand—and always in response to the most bizarre and maddening predicaments I had ever encountered.

When my husband's passport was not returned to us, and no one could tell us what had happened to it: *No problem.*

When our taxi driver missed an exit and swung a U-turn on

an eight-lane freeway, driving headlong into oncoming traffic along a narrow shoulder for a half mile: *No problem.*

When I stepped out of a hotel room into the hallway to find a solid torrent of gray-black water pouring straight through a hole as big as a dinner plate in the ceiling and rapidly flooding the hallway, the hotel employee shrugged, seeing my alarmed look: *No problem.*

When my relatives' half-built house lost power at night, turning as black as the bottom of the ocean because each gaping window frame was sealed with black plastic and no one could find a flashlight: *No problem.*

When my sister-in-law spent two hours one evening applying intricate traditional henna designs to my hands, encasing them in mud and sealing them in plastic bags and instructing me to sleep on my back like a starfish so the designs would remain intact, and then in the middle of the night I was overcome with explosive diarrhea (from food Ismail had bought from a street vendor, insisting it was *no problem* to eat) and I stumbled desperately down the pitch black hallway toward the bathroom, pawing at my pants with plastic mitts: *No problem.* I sat on the toilet, cold sweat pearling on my forehead, as my sister-in-law coaxed me from the other side of the door to let her in, reassuring me that helping me to wipe myself would be *no problem.*

That was the night I lay in bed staring up at ceiling and said flatly to Ismail: *I fucking hate this country.*

I rarely swore in the United States, but Libya brought out

a desperate, unhinged aspect of myself I usually kept carefully concealed from everyone but Ismail. Now I was swearing like a sailor to a captive audience of six relatives, the youngest of which was four. *Fuck you,* I mouthed quietly at Ismail over the heads of the children between us. Fat, furious tears spilled down my cheeks. I turned to the window, pressed my face against the cold, dirty glass, and began to sob. My sister and brother-in-law stared straight ahead, as stiff and blank-faced as crash-test dummies. The children watched us with big, curious eyes. Twelve ears were perked up and waiting to see how Ismail would respond.

I knew better than to curse Ismail. My most recent American boyfriend had been relatively unfazed by profanity; our late-night drunken arguments became swearing contests, erased from memory the following morning. But such was not the case with Ismail. His dignity was his most precious inheritance; he could not bear for it to be smeared by profanity issued from the mouth of his wife. When I called him names or provoked him by cursing, he became as incensed as a tribal warlord, willing to fight a bloody battle to reclaim his honor. My raised voice did not rile him, but a single expletive wounded him deeply and prolonged an argument for hours. I spent that time in a cold, dark place, pounding on the closed door of his heart and begging for him to feed me scraps of forgiveness.

But this time, when he turned away from me toward the window and slammed his heart shut against me, I was not alone. Still staring straight ahead, Fauziya reached behind her seat. Her hand searched for mine in my lap. She wove her fingers into my own and, with the pad of her thumb, began to stroke my palm. Like wiping dust from a window, each stroke swept away more of my anger. My breath grew steady and my head began to clear. I had imagined that Ismail was my only ally in this strange and exhausting country that was so far from my home, but I was wrong. In this moment, someone else in this cramped space understood me better than he did; someone loved me even after bearing witness to my ugliest self. Her touch told me what I needed to hear to climb out of this pit of alienation and despair. It expressed what Ismail, with his wounded pride, had never been able to say in moments like these: that I was understood, I was forgiven, and I was family.

14 | *Bartering*

The open-air market in Tripoli's Old City was a labyrinth of narrow, crowded alleys where shoppers jostled past row after row of displays: tall stacks of neatly folded cloth, a pile of shoes, a display case spilling with gold. Vendors and customers faced off in noisy negotiations, leaning over counters and slapping tabletops and jabbing the air for emphasis. A woman's slender hands appeared from a tent of cloth, and she ran them over a gold bracelet's engraving as if she were reading Braille. A fabric vendor unfurled a length of white lace with a snap of his wrist, holding it aloft only a few inches over a black puddle. As a tour guide waddled down the alley, a tight cluster of European tourists followed like skittish ducklings.

I had often tried to imagine the country where Ismail had been born and raised, the land where the Arabic trapped in his throat in our small southern town would flow as freely as it had for the first half of his life. I wanted to know him in a country where no one inquired about his strange accent within

the first few minutes of meeting him or stumbled over the pronunciation of his name. Even as our intimacy deepened back
home in North Carolina, his foreign status clung persistently
to him, permeating every aspect of our relationship, like the
spicy aroma of his clothes after he cooked a meal. Each time he
rolled an *r* across the roof of his mouth or touched his forehead
to the carpet to pray or carried on passionate phone conversations with his relatives in Libya, I was reminded how foreign
he was to me. In his native land, where I could see him not as
an immigrant but as a son and a brother, I imagined I would
finally locate the missing pieces of the puzzle.

Watching him now, maneuvering through this bustling
market in a T-shirt, jeans, baseball cap, and sandals, our
daughter balanced on his shoulders and pressing her hands
to his cheeks, I was startled by how strange he seemed here.
Never had I seen him look as American as he did surrounded
by Libyans. Men his age seemed a generation older in their
flowing white tunics and sandals. Huddled close on overturned
milk crates and plastic chairs, absorbed in animated conversations, their hands swinging dangerously close to the cups
of tea beside them, they raised their eyebrows and turned as
Ismail walked briskly past, curiosity mixed with scorn on their
faces. I suddenly understood the loneliness Ismail wore like a
second skin, the heavy judgment that landed on him wherever
he went, his nostalgia for a home that could not be found on
any map.

As we flowed along with a current of shoppers down a winding alley, we almost collided with a dwarf standing squarely in the middle of the path. Like a buoy in a stormy sea, his head bobbed in and out of view among hips and shopping bags, his thick bowed legs anchored as people elbowed past. His severely curved back forced his face toward the ground, but as we passed he cocked his head to one side and jutted his chin upward, peering up at us with what appeared to be his one good eye. In his raised fist he clutched Chinese-made children's plastic sunglasses, whose crooked plastic ends nearly collided with Ismail's chest. Aliya immediately reached for them.

"How much?" Ismail asked.

"Ten dinars!"

Ismail shot a look of disbelief at the dwarf, whose serious expression instantly melted into a placating smile. Though I couldn't speak Arabic, the counting games I had been playing with my nieces and nephews, along with the jabbing fingers and melodramatic expressions between the two men, made their negotiations easy for me to understand.

"Just for you, eight," the dwarf murmured in a lower, conspiratorial voice, glancing around him as if a stampede might ensue if other shoppers overheard this figure.

Ismail planted his feet squarely and folded his arms across the chest, towering over the dwarf, while Aliya peered down wide-eyed from his shoulders at the contest unfolding below. He shook his head emphatically. "One dinar," he countered, waving his index finger imperiously over the dwarf's head for emphasis, to show he would not be budged from this figure.

"Seven! Okay, five—no less!" the little man shrieked, his fingers fluttering, his tinny voice rising.

I glanced around, looking for anything but this argument on which to focus my attention. Nearby, a leathery-faced man in a long white tunic held a basket full of blood oranges in one hand and lifted a bag of herbs to his nose with the other. Then he dropped coins into a vendor's palm with a *clink* and walked away. I watched the white cotton sliver of his receding back until it was swallowed by the crowd. Meanwhile, like actors on the stage, Ismail and the dwarf contorted their faces from shock to outrage to cajoling smiles as they heatedly argued over what amounted to less than one dollar.

The longer I watched this baffling contest, the more anxious I became. I stared down at the thick layer of dust covering my sandals. I thought of the gleaming linoleum floors of our neighborhood grocery store, where I pushed my cart past row after row of brightly wrapped food glistening under fluorescent lights, as familiar, soothing tunes were piped into my ears like the refrigerated air that hummed through the building. I avoided eye contact with other shoppers as I maneuvered my cart past them, only barely interacting with the cashier who asked me in a monotone, without looking up from her register, if I had found what I was looking for. On days when I was too impatient to wait in line, or had an aversion to even that fleeting human contact, I chose instead to use a machine that instructed me, in an authoritative female voice, to pass my purchases over a scanner and place them into a bag. Once, a jar of spaghetti sauce had slipped through my hands and shattered on the polished white floor, spraying the red sauce across the linoleum and onto the leg of my pants. Shards of glass swam in a thick, slow-spreading puddle at my feet. Other shoppers glanced furtively up from their monitors, then tucked their chins down quickly and resumed tapping impatiently on screens, as if trying to get the attention of someone inside. The store employee bent the microphone to her mouth and spoke in a code that bounced off the polished floors. Nobody said a word to me. Shopping was as cold and efficient as swiping a credit card through a machine: no public spectacle, no unpredictable emotional exchanges, no niggling questions about fairness.

Ismail and the dwarf were still lobbing numbers back and forth like hot potatoes. Their contest may have lasted just a few minutes, but to me it felt like hours. Each imperious announcement from Ismail, each indignant shriek from the dwarf drove my blood pressure higher. I could not understand why Ismail would waste his time haggling over a few coins with someone who clearly needed the spare change far more than we did. I imagined the old man at home with his oranges by now, sitting cross-legged on the floor, lifting one to his lips, a trickle of juice dribbling onto his pristine white tunic. The light in the marketplace seemed to be changing, the sun sinking behind the buildings that bordered the narrow alleyway. And still this negotiation would not end. I tried to flash Ismail a look that said *enough,* but he was so focused on his wrangling that he didn't even notice me. Finally, I leaned into his face and mouthed, *Give. Him. The. Money.*

Ismail's eyebrows shot up in surprise. Immersed in this ancient ritual, he had momentarily forgotten all about his life on the other side of the world: his corporate job and wallet full of credit cards. His frequent flyer miles and wireless Internet access. His suburban home and his American wife.

He dug into the pocket of his shorts, pulled out a small pile of coins, and dropped them into the open palm of the dwarf, whose face broke into a victorious smile as he closed his fist over the money. He thrust a pair of sunglasses at Ismail, then retreated bowlegged and sideways through the crowd. I spun on my heels and walked briskly in the other direction.

"What's wrong?" Ismail sputtered, struggling to catch up.

I glanced back at him helplessly. *What's right?* I wanted to ask. *Can you name one thing that is right about haggling mercilessly with a disabled dwarf over forty cents in the middle of a crowded marketplace?* Instead I picked up my pace.

"You don't understand," I tossed back lamely, struggling to dislodge a single sentence from the glut of words stuck in my throat. His behavior made him seem terribly cheap and irrational; it embarrassed me. But I could see that my exasperation and judgment were just as unsettling to him, and I felt that familiar wave of exhaustion and despair as I began, once again, to search for the right words to build a bridge between us, to follow language back to this partnership, to restore us to husband and wife instead of two foreigners gaping at one another with naked prejudice.

He was nearly jogging now to keep up with me, feinting left and right to dodge approaching shoppers. I stepped up my pace, avoiding eye contact, until finally he reached for my arm and pulled me around to face him.

"Do you expect me to act like a tourist in my own hometown, to give that man exactly the price he demanded? This is what we do in the marketplace: we challenge each other. We yell. We laugh. We negotiate. It would have been an insult to him to avoid bartering. Where I come from, we don't patronize people simply because they look different."

His words were like oxygen to my smoldering resentment, fanning it into a full-blown flame. How dare he accuse me of being incapable of dealing with difference? Wasn't I here in this broken-down country on the North African coast, surrounded day and night by people who were different from me in every imaginable way? Hadn't I smiled and bowed my head, drunk and eaten everything I was offered, including the gnarled and greasy jerk meat that made my stomach turn? I'd extended my hand to yet another visitor when all I wanted was solitude. I'd spent long days and nights in crowded homes, barely feeling the sunlight on my face, when all I wanted to do was slip out the door and explore the city on my own. I'd been trying my best to play the part of gracious daughter-in-law and guest, while inside I swung among mounting resentment, dizzying boredom, and bouts of homesickness as visceral as nausea. I was beginning to feel like a marionette with a frozen smile and a bright, wooden gaze, my every gesture produced by Ismail's family and friends tugging at my strings.

And then it dawned on me: I had kept everyone here at a polite distance, had never once risked treating them like kin by engaging them in messy, authentic interactions. Not once had I clearly asserted myself or stood my ground. What would have happened if I refused another cup of tea and excused myself and disappeared behind a closed door? Or sat down next to Ismail in a room full of the men, or pulled him down beside me on the floor among the women, insisting he translate so I could have a real conversation? Instead I had approached my relatives like an anthropologist, trying my best to blend in with the surroundings while I took mental notes about their strange customs, many of which I saw through the small, sharp lens of judgment and pity.

As much as I hated to admit it, back home on American streets I would be extremely unlikely to challenge someone who was old or disabled or whose skin was a different shade than mine. I understood words like *diversity* and *tolerance* to mean white people being on their best behavior, bringing out their best manners for mostly darker-skinned others whose suffering was undeniably greater. Tolerance meant trying to understand and intuit the needs of the less privileged, like a gracious host reads the face of the shivering and hungry guest who crosses the threshold. She might very well make a mental note about the mud he dragged into the house or the mismatched clothes he wore or the fact that he showed up without an offering—but she smiled brightly and offered the best of what she had, secure in the knowledge that later he would disappear back into the dark, and this well-appointed home and all it contained would still belong to her.

In the high school I had attended in the New Mexico mountains, diversity was represented by the single black girl in our class, adopted by a white family, whose bellow and guffaw bounced off the metal lockers, and who, with her big curves, unapologetically took up as much space as a football player. Skinny white girls pressed themselves against lockers to allow her to pass and followed her with fearful, admiring eyes. Diversity was the Native American boy in stained and torn jeans and heavy-metal T-shirts, whose mane of black hair fell to his waist like a shimmering black waterfall. Tolerance meant ignoring as much as possible the black girl's blackness, ignoring, too, the fact that the Native American boy slinked into class a half hour late after hitchhiking ten miles down a mountain road from the reservation. On a winter weekend morning, my family stopped at a gas station on that same mountain road en route to a ski hill blanketed in two fresh feet of powder, and I saw him crouched on the sidewalk, eyes half-closed and chin tucked into a too-big army surplus jacket. Tolerance meant pretending not to see him and driving away.

In college, diversity meant rounding out my education by taking a literature class devoted to African novelists and another dedicated to black American writers. Our all-white class seemed to understand the unspoken rule that these authors could not be criticized or joked about. We might make offhand remarks about the long-winded ruminations of Virginia Woolf or the melancholy drama of Edgar Allen Poe, but with darker-skinned writers we grew earnest and careful, bent our heads to our desks and took copious notes, as if their writing were printed in indelible ink.

After college, when I worked at Planned Parenthood, diversity was what we encountered when we drove across the Mexican border in a van loaded with medical supplies to an ashen undercity built entirely from garbage on the outskirts of the dump. Women stared out from scrap-metal doorways. Children in cast-off clothing played with broken toys or sat in the dirt eating stale food. Our van crept past putrid puddles, barefoot children in the street, a hoarsely barking dog that appeared to be melting into a puddle of muddy blood, its lower half having been crushed by a car. As soon as I stepped from the van, a little girl ran up to me and began to sing a Madonna song. She swiveled her tiny hips and kicked up the dust with plastic flip-flops. *Los Angeles,* she said proudly, stabbing her chest with her finger, to let me know she had briefly resided in the land of the rich and famous. Smaller children circled around her, admiring the rusty scraps of English she spat into the air. Diversity was a brown palette of skin colors—from parched dust to black mud—on the bilingual birth control pamphlets we passed out that day, discreetly wiping our hands on our slacks.

Now I lived in a suburban North Carolina neighborhood, in a town known as one of the most progressive in the state. Hybrid cars whispered past the neatly manicured lawns of identical homes; gleaming white mailboxes stood at attention at precise intervals along the sidewalk. Neighbors carried on heated listserv discussions about the ethics of free-roaming cats, the effect of chicken coops on property values, organic alternatives to pesticides for the community garden. Ours was an educated, liberal American community where rainbow-colored flags billowed in doorways and residents would have more easily sworn allegiance to diversity than to the American flag—but skin color in this neighborhood was a narrow spectrum of pale, like the palette favored by the Homeowners' Association for exterior paint. Brown skin could be seen on these streets only once a month, when Spanish-speaking men in bright orange earphones marched down the street with weed cutters and leaf blowers. The residents closed their windows and drew their blinds to shut out the dust and noise. In the five years I had lived in the neighborhood, I could count on one hand the number of African Americans I had seen there: The woman who pulled into my neighbor's driveway after she left for work each Monday to clean her home. The Jehovah's Witness who appeared on my porch one hot, still afternoon in nylons and white square-heeled pumps, sweat stains darkening her polyester blouse. The men who hung off the back of the garbage truck as it made its way from house to house.

Once, at a neighborhood potluck in the cul-de-sac, I stood on a small island of grass ringed with asphalt, spooning macaroni and cheese into my mouth from a paper plate and chatting with our new neighbors. Recent retirees from California, they were clad from head to toe in pressed and immaculate white from their golf game earlier that day: pleated shorts and crisp collared shirts, bleached socks and fluffy sweatbands. Smiling broadly from beneath a visor that bore the name of a course in Maui, the woman told me she was very excited about the "diversity" in her new neighborhood. The word hung in the air between us, vibrating with hidden meaning. I felt like she was speaking to me in code; I had no idea what she was trying to say.

"I think it's a wonderful, wonderful thing," she beamed. As I listened to her, I mentally went house by house down our street, visualizing its residents: all white and middle class, every single one of them. And suddenly it dawned on me that she was referring to *my* family—to Aliya with her milky brown skin that darkened quickly in the summer. That's when I realized that my family was on the other side of this invisible line; diversity was no longer an academic exercise but a too-small box into which people would try to squeeze my children.

Ismail was right: my discomfort about his bartering in the marketplace was not just about his wrangling over such a small amount of money. It was rooted in aversion to the strange little man with the cock-eyed stare, whose back was rounded like a turtle's shell, who darted sideways like a crab through the alley. Unable to meet his one-eyed gaze, I had been nervously casting glances everywhere else: at the backs of other shoppers, at the dust hanging in the air around our ankles. So uncomfortable was I that even when he raised his voice to a shriek, I stole a quick, nervous glance only at his twisted mouth, then locked my gaze on the empty space just above his head, as if trying to erase his presence altogether. I wanted to believe that I was being compassionate and fair by giving him the price he requested, but there was another, less noble motive at play: to spend money rather than to engage a human being, to view him as a recipient of my charity rather than an equal, to use my affluence to buffer me from an unsettling world.

NOTHING ANNOYED ISMAIL more than when I reached for something in the market—fresh dates on a branch, a gauzy scarf rippling with ocean colors, the tiniest Qur'an I had ever seen—and squealed with delight, calling out to him to come and see. Never, ever should I show my enthusiasm for a purchase, he said—because my naked desire made him feel as compromised as a boxer fighting with one hand tied behind his back. One afternoon Ismail wandered into a tiny stall fully in character: a disinterested customer, keenly aware of the flaws in the gold-embroidered children's slippers on the table but possibly willing to take a couple off the vendor's hands for the right price. (He wanted to purchase one pair for Aliya and one for her friend back home.) I hung back near the hanging tapestry that marked the edge of the stall, silent and watchful. The two men sized each other up with sidelong glances as Ismail circled a table piled high with cheap slippers. Then Ismail loudly announced that purchasing two pairs entitled him to a fifty percent discount—a claim that made the shop-keeper wince and snap his neck back as if he had been struck by an invisible hand.

Over a towering pile of thin plastic soles and frayed gold thread, the two men shot offers back and forth with escalating intensity that suggested the contest had become personal. A fine, continuous spray of spittle flew through the air between them. Suddenly the vendor swung around to face me and reached out as if he would cradle my cheeks in his hands. He addressed me in heavily accented English.

"Madam, how long you are with this man?"

"Six years?"

My voice, full of insecurity, trailed off at the end. Was my uncertainty about the intimate turn of this conversation or the vow I had made to Ismail? I instantly wished I could take the words back, restate them with more confidence.

He looked at me with big, sad eyes and swung his large head slowly back and forth in pity, grunting and clucking his tongue, his leathery face creased with compassion.

"So sorry, madam. *So* sorry."

He fluttered the fingers of one hand in front of his lips, as if trying to pull at the tangled thread of words in his mouth. I watched those undulating hands like a cobra watches the slow-moving tip of the snake charmer's flute. Finally he spoke, clumsily drawing out his rusty English:

"Thirty years I am in this market . . . *thirty years!*"

With his arm raised, his index finger pointed straight up to the sky, he paused to allow me to absorb this: three decades in the dark corner of a narrow, dusty alley; thirty long years spent piling cheap shoes in precarious stacks on a wooden table and haggling over a few dollars in the hot Libyan sun.

"Never, never, *never* did I see a man like this." He leveled his index finger at Ismail's chest like a victim identifies a criminal in a courtroom. Ismail watched our exchange, smiling and unfazed, looking very much like a wise man or an idiot.

The vendor locked eyes with me. His black eyes drilled straight into mine, into the darkest center where I kept my secret heartache. When two people commit their lives to one another, Americans offer champagne and bath towels, kitchen appliances and well wishes in flowery script. But this was the very first time someone had offered me pity or sympathy for predicament of my marriage, had ever acknowledged the suffering contained in this difficult union. I felt totally exposed. This man could see all the secrets I carried: my petty misunderstandings and accumulated resentments, the lonely nights I lay on the narrow edge of my bed, tense and sleepless.

On those nights I lay utterly still, face to the window, as Ismail slept. Through a crack in the curtain my neighbor's back porch light shone like a lighthouse beacon, just beyond reach of this turbulent marriage, where colliding expectations led to towering waves of loneliness and despair. I stared at that small, bright light and wondered about our neighbors: high school sweethearts from a small town only a couple of hours away. They had attended the same university; during basketball season they wore matching jerseys and hung the flag of their alma mater on their porch. Each October they propped on their lawn a scarecrow in a rakish straw hat, and it beamed at us with relentless good cheer each time we passed by. Its smile was as bright and unchanging as our neighbors' when we saw them weeding the lawn together, heading to the gym in matching nylon sweatsuits, or sharing sections of the newspaper on their porch on weekend mornings. In December they emerged bundled in sweaters to follow one another around their small yard, one holding lengths of plastic green wire aloft while the other navigated around the bushes, stringing small colorful lights over each prickly shrub that bordered their walkway.

They looked like brother and sister—their pink-white skin painted from the same canvas, their identical accents creating a harmony of soprano and bass lines. It must be so much easier, I imagined, to pair up like two of a kind on Noah's ark, to choose a mate cut from the same cloth and to pave a future smooth as asphalt, covering so much common ground: faith, food, television shows, politics, hobbies, humor.

When Ismail's behavior was particularly maddening to me, I told myself that cultural differences were the source of our misunderstandings. It comforted me to imagine that even when he seemed the most impossible to understand, his behavior made sense somewhere very far away, on the other side of the world. But now I was seized with a terrifying thought: what if he was in fact maddening on *both* sides of the world?

Seeing my worried expression, Ismail said something to the vendor in Arabic, and the two men looked from one another to me and burst into laughter, shaking their heads like old friends with a long-running joke between them.

To me, it seemed unbearably intimate to engage a stranger this way, eye-to-eye and countering his demands with my own; it was hard enough to do this with my most close-knit relationships. I'd spent the last six years waiting impatiently, and with mounting disappointment, for Ismail to decipher longings that I expressed as a lingering gaze, a crestfallen look, a pregnant silence. I thought that was the way true love was supposed to work: if he adored me, if he stared deeply enough into my eyes, he would understand desires I couldn't articulate or even fully understand myself. After so many missed cues, off-base assumptions, and cyclical arguments, we were finally learning to convey our needs and desires to each other—in a fumbling and awkward way, like stiff-legged toddlers who stumble and jerk as they take their first halting steps forward.

But in the marketplace, Ismail showed no trepidation, no doubt or misunderstanding. He faced vendors squarely, engaging them intuitively in a dance of challenge and compromise: pressing and yielding, voices rising and falling, until the balance of power was reached and a deal could be struck. I wanted to learn to speak that language.

15 | *Covering*

After my first few days in Libya, I recognized a pattern: at any home we visited, Ismail would stay by my side for the introductions, then disappear into another room with the men and leave me alone with my female relatives for hours. If I went in desperation to find him, I faced the critical stares of patriarchs who could not believe my audacity to have entered the men's room and interrupted their conversation. They scowled at Ismail like restaurant patrons do at the parents of poorly behaved children, silently imploring him to take control of his charge. So instead I stayed put. Here, there would be no escape for hours, so I tried to surrender to my circumstances. The circle of women closed around me like a tent. I took a deep breath and studied the hands around me—refilling a teacup, resting on a thigh, tucking a strand of hair beneath a head scarf. I listened to the rustle of long dresses and smelled something buttery and sweet in the oven.

In the United States I spent most daylight hours in an office tapping on a keyboard until my wrists ached. I equated travel with being outside—surfing waves, walking city streets, hiking narrow mountain paths—and I had looked forward to spending my vacation in the sun, exploring Libya. But nearly all my time in Ismail's native country would be spent inside the crowded homes of women who called me sister, aunt, or daughter. While other foreigners took guided tours of Roman ruins or were whisked into the desert on air-conditioned buses, I sat thigh-to-thigh with my relatives at social gatherings that often lasted as long as an entire workday. Hours and days slipped past in a blur as I lounged on floor pillows, lulled into a stupor by the steady hum of Arabic, the whistle of boiling water, the tinkle of porcelain and laughter.

The women chatted and stared at me with naked curiosity while I smiled politely and sipped my syrupy-sweet green tea out of a tiny glass cup, never understanding a word that was spoken. One day, while I sat with these women for five hours straight, a twisting in my gut forced me to rise abruptly and step over them as I rushed to the bathroom. As I sat on the toilet, the cold, damp tile soaking through my socks, I heard a whispered conference outside the thin door. The knob gently turned and a hand appeared through the crack in the door, offering me first slippers, then toilet paper. When I emerged several minutes later, curious faces turned toward me in unison to stare. I returned to my place among them on the floor, mute and miserable, the gurgle and groan of my stomach my only contribution to the conversation.

Watching my mother-in-law raise herself slowly from the

floor and shuffle into the kitchen, I felt sorry for her and her daughters. Their days passed mostly in these cramped rooms; their lives revolved in a tight orbit around their families and their faith. They would never know the thrill of boarding an airplane alone for a destination they'd never seen; they'd never have a credit card in their name or enjoy the endorphin rush of a hard workout. My long runner's legs jutted like sharp outcroppings among the soft hills of their bodies. Back home, my hips were too broad to fit into designer jeans, but Hajja was right: in Libya I was far too skinny. None of the women I encountered were as angular as I was. I'd taken up running in college in Southern California after I'd tried to tamp down my homesickness and anxiety in the cafeteria with bowl after bowl of pasta and ice cream and sugary cereal. The fifteen pounds I'd quickly gained horrified me, and I began to run each morning along the edge of the Pacific, my feet sinking heavily into the sand. I ran until my chest heaved and my legs turned rubbery, until I doubled over to catch my breath. I ran until I no longer felt the fear that pressed against my rib cage like a tumor. Running had been my religion ever since, my path to a fleeting sense of peace and well-being. I'd run through painful breakups, cross-country moves, the completion of a master's thesis, and a persistent longing I couldn't name.

As far as I could tell, the only exercise routine my sisters-in-law maintained was their five daily prayers, when they stood erect, then bent at the waist, then knelt and prostrated on the floor, placing their foreheads on the ground facing Mecca. Yet somehow without the benefit of daily aerobic exercise, they glowed as if endorphins coursed through their veins. Curled up on floor pillows like cats, their low laughter a contented purr, they were far more relaxed than my fit and toned girl-friends back home, who needed at least one drink to unwind this much.

"You're too skinny! Eat!" Ismail whispered in my ear late at night, gently pinching my thigh and pulling me closer to him beneath the covers. He was teasing, but I knew that deep down he agreed with his mother. I had always known him to be ef-fusive with his compliments, but his praise of my figure often included a baffling invitation.

"I love every inch of your body," he might say. Then, after a brief pause: "And I sure would love more of it to hold on to — ten, even twenty, more pounds. Anytime you feel like relaxing and spreading out a bit, you go right ahead." He'd wink and smile, and I'd stare at him in mute confusion. Growing up in California in the seventies, I learned to define feminine beauty as bronzed supermodels with bellies as taut as drums. I thought women were supposed to be light as air, diaphanous as angels, luminous and lean. But these round Libyan women, so solidly planted on the earth, were undeniably lovely. Their soft, con-cealed bodies; their bright, open faces; their infectious laugh-ter and big gestures; their calm, inviting presence redefined loveliness for me. Watching them, I finally understood how Ismail defined beauty.

My mother-in-law, Hajja, kept close watch over me, her one good eye meeting my gaze while the other cloudy, unseeing one stared over my shoulder into the distance. Her eye was irreparably damaged from a beating she sustained at the hands of Ismail's father—a violation that my husband was still unable to forgive decades later. He told me his illiterate mother, with her wall-eyed gaze and her weathered, tattooed face, was brilliant—that she was the reason he had made it all the way to the United States to earn his doctorate. Each night when he was a child, his father returned from the market stall where he worked and dropped an oily, wrinkled paper bag full of that day's earnings onto the floor where the family was gathered. Each night, Hajja stole a small handful of bills from that bag and stashed them in her room, saving the spare change to buy pieces of gold, which she then squirreled away until her children needed them most.

Though she had never even learned to read, she was determined that each of her four daughters would finish college. When her daughters were students at the university, she cajoled neighbors and friends into driving her across town to campus so she could introduce herself to their professors and inquire about their academic progress. When Ismail was a teenager doing his mandatory service in the Libyan army, his mother convinced a neighbor to chaperone her to the military barracks so she could visit him. She approached the gates cradling her newborn son close to her chest: the last of thirteen children she delivered. Middle-aged by then, she shuffled down the road like a grandmother. Nearly two decades of childbirth, nursing, parenting, and grieving lost children had aged her physically, creased her face, and collapsed her shoulders into the weight of her heavy breasts. But she was also steely-eyed and fearless, as tough on the inside as a street fighter. She stopped at an iron gate where a sullen army officer sat in a plastic bucket seat in a small room.

"I'm here to see my son," she announced, shifting the slight weight of the newborn on her chest.

"No visitors," the army officer barked. He waved her off like a mosquito without even looking at her.

"I need to see him. I'm here to show him his newborn brother," Hajja insisted, planting her feet and straightening her shoulders.

"No visitors. Go home!"

When she raised her voice and reiterated her demand once more through the narrow window, he leapt from his chair and exploded through the door, kicking and swatting at her like a stray dog. She shielded her infant with her arms and backed away as he hurled limbs and insults at her. She found refuge from the blistering sun in a nearby drainage ditch, where she sat cross-legged and fuming with her baby until her neighbor returned to deliver her home. She never forgot the face or name of that army officer, a petty Gaddafi man from her hometown. More than three decades later, during the uprising, she called us at home in North Carolina to report triumphantly that he had panicked and fled the country like a dog with its tail between its legs.

Ismail often wondered what his mother might have accomplished if she had been born into a different culture, a different era, a different country. They had a running joke between them: when she shared her opinions about the world with Ismail, and he complimented her intelligence, she held up her thumb and pointer finger as if to measure a tiny sliver of air. "If only I had the tiniest bit of education—just this much—I would have been unstoppable," she would say.

Hajja flew in a plane only twice in her life: to Riyadh, Saudi Arabia, to perform the Hajj—the Muslim pilgrimage to Mecca—and to Italy, an hour-long flight over the Mediterranean, to visit her sister whose husband worked briefly at the Libyan embassy in Rome. She spent her first day ever outside Libya wandering down narrow Italian cobblestone streets. When she grew tired, she squatted down on the sidewalk and drew her thin cloth over her head to rest. A few moments later she heard a sound like a tiny metallic raindrop—*plink*—hitting the ground nearby. Then another, and another. A few coins rolled across the cobblestone and settled near her feet, and she realized that the Italians walking past assumed she was a beggar. When Hajja told me this story, she slapped her hand on her thigh, threw her head back, and laughed, her gold tooth glinting in the light.

Late one evening, exhausted and jet-lagged, I excused myself from a large social gathering in the main room and retreated to Hajja's bedroom, where I lay down on a thin cushion on the floor. Just as I closed my eyes, the door squeaked open and she padded quietly into the room. Her joints creaked and popped as she gathered her dress around her and lowered herself to the ground by my head. I opened my eyes to see her smiling at me from only inches away.

A rush of panic came over me as I squeezed my eyes shut. The strange language, the foreign smells and tastes, the social gatherings that lasted longer than a full workday—these aspects of Libya I had been able to handle. But a mother-in-law who sat only inches from my face watching me sleep—this I did not think I could bear. In my family, we considered personal space to be sacred. At family gatherings we tiptoed carefully around one another, ever fearful of becoming an imposition. Firmly believing the adage that fish and visitors stank after three days, we limited our visits to weekends—even when we flew across the entire country to see one another, even when we hadn't seen one another in months. As guests in one another's homes, we pounced on the first opportunity to clean a dish or clear a table, anything to minimize the burden of our presence. And we never, ever opened closed doors.

After a few moments, I heard a long sigh and the soft rustling of cloth. I opened my eyes to see Hajja first rubbing her tired eyes and then tugging loose the thin head scarf she had worn since my arrival. She swept it from her head, and long, spindly strands of hair came tumbling down around her face. To my great surprise, her hair was an electric red—a rich, playful, utterly unexpected color. Noticing my wide-eyed look of surprise, Hajja began to laugh—an explosive cackle that opened up her face and shook her pendulous breasts in her lap. Pointing to her hair, she repeated one of the few Arabic words I understood: *henna*. I nodded and reached out to touch a long strand that had fallen across her shoulder. Her hair was as silken as a child's. I wrapped a strand around my fingers while Hajja held my gaze, smiling. All my awkwardness, all my resistance to the strange and relentless intimacy of this place, disappeared.

During my last week in Libya, my sisters-in-law insisted on dressing me in traditional clothing. With my eyes closed, I felt fingertips sweep through my hair as someone brushed it; I felt warm breath on my cheek as someone else stroked eyeshadow gently over my lids. My sisters-in-law spent hours decorating my feet and hands with intricate henna designs. No one stopped to answer a text message, make a phone call, or check email. No one grew antsy because she needed to run errands or get to the gym or have time to herself. Each gave her time and attention lavishly, as if these precious resources flowed through her blood like the oil that coursed beneath the Libyan desert. I drank in the intimacy in the room, and it warmed me from the inside, loosened the tension in my neck, turned time into something warm and fluid, in which I was completely submerged.

Seeing the faces of my sisters-in-law crowded around mine, I was overcome for the first time with envy. I could not imagine living as they did, confined mostly to their homes and subject to the will of their husbands—and yet I ached for the intimacy they shared, for their selfless generosity, for their abiding faith and the slow pace of their daily lives, devoid of my typically American concerns: balancing career and family, saving for retirement, trying to stay fit and thin. They would never experience the freedoms I enjoyed, but neither would they have to correspond with their closest relatives by email from thousands of miles away. They would never negotiate eight weeks' maternity leave with a boss who viewed that arrangement as generous or leave their tiny babies with a stranger for eight hours while they sat in an office across town. They would never worry that the lines on their face made them less marketable in a tough economy. They would never know the persistent sense of failure or the creeping despair that comes from doggedly chasing the elusive dream that women can be everything at once: sexy and youthful, independent and financially successful, extraordinary mothers and wives.

They turned me in circles, wrapping stiff, gold-embroidered cloth around my body, then covered my head in even more cloth and girded my neck with an ornate gold necklace that hung all the way to my waist. I liked to wear clothes that showed off my best features (long legs, narrow waist) and minimized my worst ones (small chest, big bottom). But beneath these concealing layers of cloth, my body was no longer divided into good and bad parts; it was a seamless whole. I had always equated feeling sexy with feeling beautiful, but swaddled in this material I felt entirely different: hidden and safe.

When Ismail stepped into the room, I felt silly and self-conscious, as if I were in costume, but his face registered awe, not amusement. "You look beautiful," he whispered. How could I, when there was so little of me to be seen? But when my sisters-in-law led me to a mirror, I understood what he meant: All that colorful, shimmering cloth caught the light as it fell sensually to the floor, and in the midst of it my face shone as fresh and inviting as a blossoming flower. With no other part of my body to appraise, I met my own gaze in the mirror. I barely recognized my expression: not the anxious frown of a tourist but the relaxed smile of someone who felt at home.

16 | *Escape*

Though my in-laws did everything they could to make me feel welcome in their homes, I would never be at ease in Muammar Gaddafi's Libya. Entering the country was like stepping inside the ransacked home of an abuser, where suffering was written on the faces of everyone I saw. Everything showed signs of neglect: the sidewalks strewn with trash, the potholes big enough to swallow a tire, the buildings whose gaping window frames offered no protection from the wind. Those who live in a violent home know that a separate weather system exists beneath its roof; it sits under a gathering storm cloud even when the sun is shining. Those who live under a tyrant learn to tread lightly and to sniff the air for the scent of danger: muscles quivering and tensed for flight, studying the faces of loved ones for signs of peril. In Gaddafi's Libya, people inhaled fear along with oxygen, and as it saturated their bloodstream, it caused paranoid, racing thoughts; a disorienting lethargy; and a tendency to choke on words. There was no escape from the heavy weight of oppression.

My chest had tightened as soon as I saw the towering portrait of Gaddafi as I exited the plane. In his 1970s-era sunglasses, with what looked like a coonskin cap on his head and a flowing scarf around his neck, he loomed so high above us that we stared up into his broad nostrils on our way to customs. Ismail translated the Arabic inscription beneath the portrait for me: BROTHER GADDAFI, OUR SOULS BELONG TO YOU.

"You must understand, Krista," my brother-in-law Adel explained later, as we stepped gingerly over patches of crabgrass in an abandoned field near his home, "this country has been run by a psychotic leader for so long that all Libyans suffer from mental illness." Ahead of us, Aliya hid in a small cluster of palm trees—the closest thing to a playground we could find. Adel spoke more freely in that barren field than he did in the privacy of his own home--as if his words were too dangerous to be uttered inside. "Our mental illness comes from having to tell so many lies to ourselves and others just to survive another day," he said. Even the smallest criticisms of the regime led to disappearances, prolonged incarceration without legal representation, or torture. An enormous amount of pretending was required to try to lead a normal life.

A gaunt man with square, outdated glasses and the broad, lopsided smile of a boy, Adel was an electrical engineer who worked for the military. The best year of his life, he said, was the one he spent in the former Yugoslavia, pursuing his master's degree. On our first night at his home, he showed us pictures of his simple, well-lit apartment in Belgrade, with its kitchen cabinets full of food; the manicured parks in which he and his new young wife strolled each weekend; the beautiful, well-maintained architecture of the city. His favorite stories about Yugoslavia recalled freedoms so familiar to me that I no longer recognized them as such: the dinner parties they hosted for Yugoslavian friends, during which heated political debates took place at the table and laughter filled their apartment until late into the night; the evenings his wife slipped out of the apartment to wander the city alone and clear her head. At thirty-six, Adel had only one dream: to experience life outside Libya once more. But like an old man who mumbles wistfully about the past, he spoke as if he knew his dream was beyond reach.

In spite of everything Libyans had lost during more than four decades of Gaddafi's brutal reign—freedom of speech and movement, freedom to access basic goods or to improve one's life—they remained rich in their connections to one another. The day we had arrived in Ismail's hometown, a steady stream of friends and family passed through my father-in-law's home, warmly welcoming Ismail and inspecting his American wife and daughter. And each day we were there, many more neighbors and relatives visited. Yet Gaddafi had turned their most precious resource against them: every Libyan knew that to speak out against Gaddafi was to put loved ones in Libya at risk, which is why even Libyans living abroad were afraid to challenge the regime. There was nowhere on earth they could escape their bondage to Gaddafi.

In the evenings Adel played me his favorite music: Johnny Cash, Merle Haggard, Kenny Rogers. As we listened to country music, Adel told me stories about his life. He loved to watch my brow furrow in confusion or my eyes widen with disbelief as he described life under "the brother leader." Maybe it was a relief for him to see the truth written across my face.

Take his story of purchasing a car. One Friday afternoon, an announcement was made at the military office where he worked: any employee who wanted to purchase a vehicle must bring a down payment of two thousand dinars to his or her supervisor the following Monday, because the government was expecting a shipment of cars from across the Mediterranean. Like most of his colleagues, Adel had nowhere near enough money, so he spent his weekend frantically contacting friends and family, securing small cash loans for this rare opportunity. On Monday morning he handed his supervisor a thick envelope stuffed with cash.

Two years later, when the long-awaited car shipment finally arrived, he spent a day at the port watching other government employees drive away in gleaming new Volkswagen Jettas, until there were no more cars to be distributed. A year after that he was summoned back to the port and presented with a shiny red

Tata—the Indian version of a Yugo—a car not much bigger than a golf cart. He never asked why it took more than three years for his car to arrive or why some colleagues who paid the same amount as he did received a Jetta. To inquire about the injustice would have been unwise.

As his story drew to a close, Adel began to laugh at my shocked expression. His wife, Fauziya, joined in, and so did Ismail. They held their foreheads and chuckled, their laughter increasing each time they caught my gaze, until their bellies shook and their eyes watered. Pretty soon I was laughing, too—but my amusement was barbed with guilt and sorrow, because I knew it wouldn't be long before I would return to my hometown, where car dealerships lined the freeway and I could purchase almost any make or model I wanted for no money down. Adel and his family would remain in Libya, with his tiny Tata locked up in his garage, this car he could not afford to drive except on special occasions because his only investment in his family's future was to sell it as a rare commodity in Libya.

Gaddafi followed me everywhere I went—peering down from billboards lining the highway, dangling from the rearview mirror of taxis, accosting me in hotel lobbies and restaurants. Each street was marked with Gaddafi's signature green: doors, lampposts, window frames of otherwise stately buildings that recalled Italy's colonial presence. At a museum filled with artifacts of the Roman Empire, I found a marble bust of Gaddafi standing conspicuously beside one of a Roman emperor. One day, as we passed a large mural bearing his profile, my daughter turned to me abruptly. "Is that man a movie star?" she asked, pointing to his cartoonish face. Then she screwed up her face with distaste. "I'm glad we don't have that movie star at home, Mom. He's not handsome at all—and he doesn't look funny, either."

Later, Ismail translated as I shared this story with my mother-in-law. We were seated on the floor drinking syrupy green tea; only the four of us were at home. Her hand flew reflexively to her face to hide her smile, and then, for the only time during our visit, she fixed me with a severe expression. In a forceful whisper, with her finger pressed to her lips, she admonished me to never, ever speak this way in Libya again.

When Ismail asked me what I thought of his homeland, I tried to choose my words carefully, knowing how much he loved this country and its people, how desperately he wanted me to see its beauty. He'd told me stories about the pristine beaches of his hometown, but all I saw were decrepit buildings along a littered coastline. He'd told me stories about celebrations that filled the streets, about falling asleep to the sound of drumming and chanting, about women who cooked feasts big enough to feed an entire village. But I saw only barren homes, empty cabinets lacking basic necessities, and subdued women. So I learned to lie. I never admitted that the country he loved existed only in his imagination or that I could not find a moment of peace in Gaddafi's shadow or that his family's desperate generosity filled me with sadness. I never told Ismail that under Gaddafi his homeland had become a prison, and that as long as he remained in power, I never wanted to return to this country. How could I tell him I would not allow his children to maintain a relationship with their Libyan family?

Ismail's passport was finally returned to us. After Ismail had spent weeks inquiring with government officials, his brother showed up one day and handed it over, never explaining its disappearance or how it had arrived on his doorstep. The day before we left Libya, Ismail's mother and sisters sat in a tight circle and wailed as if they were at a funeral. Their tears flowed on and on, and I knew that as much as they loved us, they were grieving for themselves as well. The next day we would pack our suitcases, flash our passports, and soar away to a different world, abandoning them to this one. Though I tried to conceal my feelings, I couldn't wait to leave; in spite of their extraordinary hospitality, ever since we had arrived in this country, I had felt increasingly desperate to escape.

The morning of our flight, Adel and Fauziya stood outside their home, their arms crossed against their chests, their shoulders curled inward. I did not want to say good-bye, so instead I told them I would see them in Europe one day; that we would reunite in the former Yugoslavia and they would guide me through the streets of Belgrade. Adel smiled weakly, and then he reached out for Fauziya and clung to her as if, without her support, the slightest wind could topple him.

None of us dreamed that morning that Adel would leave Libya in only a few short years. The last time I spoke to him, over the crackling of a faulty phone line, he told me he had been ill for quite some time. Several Libyan doctors had failed to diagnose his cancer, and in spite of the country's massive oil wealth, Libyan medical facilities were not equipped to provide the treatment he needed. He spent the following months navigating the Libyan bureaucracy, filing paperwork for a travel visa, awaiting permission to travel, and preparing to undergo chemotherapy abroad. By the time he finally arrived in Jordan several months later, found an apartment, and began treatment, it was too late for him. Just before he died, he'd been trying to get back to Libya to spend his last days with those he loved.

The morning we left Libya, we said good-bye to Ismail's family in the crowded living room of his parents' home. Only his father followed us out to the narrow dirt alley behind his house, where a taxi idled beside a concrete wall, waiting to take us to the airport. He was wrapped in a long white cloth like a toga, its bright white hem floating inches above the mud. He had just returned from the mosque. He put his hand over his heart to say good-bye and then, as we squeezed into the backseat of the taxi, he leaned down at the open window and began to chant in a low murmur. "He's praying for our protection," Ismail whispered beside me. His blessing hung in the air between us, and I imagined it drifting back out the open window and staying behind with our loved ones in Libya.

III | *Homecoming*

17 | *Betrayal*

A month after we returned from Libya, an ultrasound technician handed me a small black-and-white picture of a baby with a tiny penis. I squinted at the hazy image, then turned it sideways and reexamined it in the bright light of the hospital corridor. Until that moment, I had felt like a babushka doll, hiding within me a smaller version of myself. I had imagined tiny ovaries growing next to my own, a tiny womb somewhere inside of mine. I was raised in a family of four girls. When my sisters and I are together, we speak a private language composed largely of different pitches of laughter that causes our exasperated father to demand to know what's so funny. I am most at home when I am sharing clothes, secrets, and a bathroom with other women. So when I became pregnant for the second time, I looked forward to giving my five-year-old daughter a sister. It was difficult for me to accept that I was carrying a boy.

With the women in my family I felt porous—as if I absorbed

their thoughts and feelings through my very own skin. They did not have to tell me they were angry or excited, nervous or depressed; I could feel it in the way they held my gaze, in the spaces between the words they spoke. Five years after her birth, my daughter and I remained tethered to one another by an invisible cord through which her moods coursed straight into my bloodstream. But with men it was different: their skin coarse and impenetrable, their expressions blunt or inscrutable. I stumbled into moments of intimacy with Ismail that were startling and unexpected; no sooner had I felt them than I began to feel the loss of him as he retreated back into his separate world. It seemed we were always in a state of approach or retreat, moving toward or away from one another, our intimacy a moving target.

A few weeks after we discovered I was carrying a boy, Ismail and I invited a friend to dinner who casually asked us if we intended to have our son circumcised. To me, the answer was obvious. We had just prepared a detailed birth plan with our midwife, outlining a strategy to cushion our son's transition into this world: the lights in the birthing room would be low; my baby would rest on my chest immediately after birth; he would stay with us at all times in the hospital. Why would we go to such lengths to minimize trauma and then subject him to a painful and unnecessary procedure? As I shook my head, I was astonished to see Ismail nodding on the other side of the table. It had never occurred to me that he might have a different opinion, though it should have, since he'd been raised according to Muslim traditions.

But Ismail had reinvented himself when he had moved to the United States; he'd cast off the outward signs of his background—the style of dress, the diet, the language—and transformed himself from a traditional North African Muslim into a progressive middle-class American. He relished his new freedom to openly date women, to jog down the street in running shorts, to protest the government. But some traditions can't be discarded as easily as a wardrobe or a cuisine; not even Ismail knew that circumcision was in his blood until he discovered he had fathered a son.

Ismail had rejected those aspects of Arab culture that seemed most oppressive. He had explosive arguments with his father in which he defended his sisters' right to choose their own husbands, and years later he admonished those husbands to help their wives with the household duties. While the rest of the men sat waiting to be served, Ismail insisted on working side by side in the kitchen with the women in his family. He was skeptical about the oppressive aspects of American culture as well: debt, for example, which he feared would make him an indentured servant to corporations. He objected to American standards of feminine beauty, which encouraged women to develop eating disorders or have plastic surgery to conform to the culture's unrealistic expectations. He refused to be defined by his job, and he struggled to maintain a balance among work, home, and community. Given all of this, I found his position on circumcision as nonsensical as demanding a dowry for our daughter on her wedding day.

"Why on earth would you want your son to be circumcised?" I asked Ismail, unable to suppress the judgment and incredulity in my voice. Our guest had left, and we were in the kitchen. I was loading the dishwasher, and he was wiping the counters.

"Because it's what the men in my family do," he replied curtly.

"Yes, but *why?*" I turned to face him and crossed my arms over my chest, awaiting his response, but he refused to meet my gaze. Instead he kept his eyes locked on the counter as he wiped in slow, thoughtful circles. He had no answer. My practical husband, the scientist who trusted reason more than intuition, the one who had shaken off so much of his oppressive background, was inexplicably tied to this particular ritual from his past.

Ismail believed that the truth was verifiable and that disputes could be resolved by studying the facts. When we disagreed, he often prefaced his strongest argument with the phrase "The bottom line is . . ." He said these four words with absolute confidence, as if he were standing on rock-solid ground. I found his certainty maddening. To me, the truth was not solid, but liquid: it slipped easily through my fingers, reflected the light in different ways, and took the shape of the countless perspectives that tried to contain it. Because he liked to back up his arguments with data, Ismail often concluded with "I'll send you some links." The next day he'd email me his online sources.

And so in my efforts to protect our unborn son's penis, I borrowed his strategy. I printed stacks of articles about the drawbacks of circumcision for Ismail to read, confident that once I'd educated him, he would change his mind. He piled these articles by his bedside and read them one by one, his brow furrowed, while I lay in bed beside him, studying his face as he read.

"What do you think?" I pressed him after he finished an article that detailed the pain of the procedure and the future potential for diminished sexual pleasure. He put the article down and rubbed his eyes.

"I want my son to be circumcised," he said simply, shrugging his shoulders.

"In Arabic we call it *tahara,* which means 'purification,'" he explained. "For Muslims, this is a way to follow in the footsteps of the prophet Muhammad. It is an honor and a rite of passage."

"Should my son also follow in the Prophet's footsteps by being illiterate? By having multiple wives? By sleeping on a rough mat and giving away whatever coins he finds in his house at the end of each day?" My voice was rising; the conversation was deteriorating rapidly.

No scientific study or public-health message could change Ismail's mind. Circumcision was what men in his family did, and he needed his son to be a part of that lineage. He made me feel that if I prevented the procedure, I would be breaking one of his last and most important connections to his heritage.

Part of me wanted to honor my husband's wishes. Over the course of our marriage, Ismail had accepted many of my idiosyncrasies: my difficulty with apologies, my desire to sit down and write rather than clean house, my need to disappear alone into the woods to clear my head. He didn't ask me to back up these behaviors with data. Instead he watched our daughter when I disappeared. And when I returned, rather than waiting for the apologies he deserved, he broke the tension by reaching for my hand. He accepted me in spite of the fact that I confounded him, and I felt I should do the same for him. But I also wanted to protect our son.

One day, as we were leaving our couples therapy, I offhandedly asked our secular Jewish therapist if he'd had his own sons circumcised. "Of course," he said without hesitation. But like my husband, he could not provide a clear explanation for why he had done so, though he did offer that the circumcised penis was more "attractive." He and my husband nodded knowingly at each other. Ismail and I had spent many hours in this therapist's office, and this man, so adept at analyzing the subtle ways in which we caused each other pain—our tone of voice, our choice of words, our avoidance—now spoke as if cutting away the most sensitive part of a baby's body made perfect sense and required no further consideration.

At the end of one of my last prenatal visits, just after my midwife had finished measuring my belly, I asked if she knew where I could get my son circumcised. I may as well have asked her for a cigarette. She stared at me long and hard, as if she suddenly didn't recognize me. Then she began to tell me in slow, measured tones that the procedure was not medically necessary. She pointed out that it was no longer covered by some insurance policies; by the time my son was in high school, more than half of his peers would be uncut. She talked about hygiene and sexual satisfaction. She even told me about support groups for men who mourned the loss of their foreskins and about kits men purchased on the Internet to help regrow them. She asked me to consider this decision very carefully.

NOTHING COULD HAVE prepared me for the sight of my newborn son naked, his penis curled like an inchworm on the bright red apple of his swollen scrotum. The skin of his genitals was glistening and raw and appeared so paper thin that I worried it would tear at the lightest touch. It seemed to me like a defect: such vulnerable organs exposed rather than shielded beneath muscle and bone, and for the first few days I avoided touching these parts of him entirely.

But before long I became intimate with the male body in a way I never had been before. As a young woman I'd regarded men's bodies as a dangerous neighborhood I rushed through in the dark, heart pounding, eyes closed tight. Once, in my early twenties, after I'd had a lover for several months, I'd caught sight of his penis in the morning light and gasped in alarm. "You're not circumcised—I can't believe it!" He'd replied with equal alarm, "And I can't believe it took you so many months to discover that!"

With my newborn son, Khalil, I came to know the male body as precious and vulnerable. I was falling in love with his soft apricot ears, his tiny red toes, his sweet, milky scent—and, yes, his penis. Intoxicated by a mother's love, I saw every part of him as perfect. One day, sitting in a cafe with Khalil curled against my chest, I looked around and thought: each man in this room was once this small and pure. My eyes grew damp as I studied the barista pouting over the espresso machine, his faded jeans slung low on his hips; at the elderly man in the corner hunched over a newspaper; at the gregarious college boys clustered at the next table. I felt a surge of tenderness toward them all.

My arguments with Ismail about circumcision were the only dark shadow in the early weeks of Khalil's life. Our discussions unsettled me; normally compassionate and open-minded, Ismail became like a stubborn patriarch. When I offered what I thought were compelling reasons to forgo circumcision—the trauma, the risk, the unnecessary violation of our son's body— he stared blankly at me, as if I were speaking a foreign language. Up against hundreds of years of Muslim tradition, my arguments felt flimsy and disposable, like cheap plastic up against concrete. I was being worn down. Inside my head I heard the voices of my own ancestors, especially the women, whispering that there was no other option than to submit to his male authority, that a wife's role was to honor her husband's will.

One day a mother on the playground told me that her two sons had been circumcised by a wonderful Jewish doctor who had come to their home, used anesthesia, and allowed the father to hold their baby during the brief procedure. She said that he was very skillful. "In fact," she added in a confidential tone and with a touch of pride, "several doctors have commented to me about what a good job he did." I wondered what an exceptionally well-circumcised penis looked like.

But I was encouraged by the idea of doing it in our own home, that my son would not be strapped onto a "circumcision board," which looked like a neonatal torture device. So one morning, with my sleeping son curled against my chest, I called the doctor the woman at the playground had recommended. A receptionist answered the phone.

"I need to make an appointment for a circumcision," I said nervously. "I was hoping . . ."

"Can you please hold?" she replied in a bright monotone that made me wonder briefly if she was human or digitized. The line clicked and then tinny, vaguely familiar classical music was piped into my ears. I ran my fingers along my baby's back and toyed with the idea of hanging up. A moment later she was back on the line, thanking me for my patience.

"I'd like to schedule a circumcision to be done at my home," I said nervously. Her reply was brisk.

"Is your son Jewish?"

And then: "I'm sorry, ma'am, but our doctor only performs house calls for Jewish babies. If you'll hold for just a moment longer, I'll schedule an office visit."

Sitting on hold, cradling the phone between my cheek and my shoulder, I looked at the baby sleeping at my breast. Khalil was too young and pure to belong to any religion. He was *all* of them. But I was exhausted by this conflict that had hovered over my marriage for months. I wanted to accept Ismail as he had always accepted me. And I needed to put this discord behind us. If this was going to be done, I wanted it done quickly. When I was connected with the receptionist, I made the first available appointment.

The doctor's office was located in a complex that also housed a tax accountant and a real-estate broker. We arrived early. I stood glumly behind two others in line waiting to check in. Each step forward added to my misery. When it was my turn, a ruddy-faced receptionist with pink lip gloss smiled sweetly up at me.

"Don't worry, mama—your baby will be just fine," she reassured me in the same soft southern accent I had heard on the phone. I nodded, my eyes welling with tears, but her words were no more comforting than an inscription on a Hallmark card. On the wall behind her hung a framed picture of George W.

Bush, along with an inscription thanking the doctor for his contributions to the Republican Party. In the movies, bad things happened in dark places, with skewed camera angles and ominous music playing in the background, but in real life suffering was often perpetuated in locales like this waiting room with its soothing music and color-coordinated furniture.

The nurse called my son's name, and I handed him to Ismail. I was able to give my permission for him to be cut but not to be there with him while it happened. I sat on a small chair in the hallway, sobbing into my hands when I heard Khalil scream (in response to the injection of anesthetic, I later found out). I wanted to rip the pictures off the walls; to howl at the receptionist, who smiled blandly at me from her station; to claw my way through the door to the examining room. My heart pounded against my ribs. It felt as if I sat doubled over in that seat for a very long time, but the procedure lasted less than five minutes.

After it was over, when I heard my husband call my name, I rushed into the room—a histrionic and tardy savior—and grabbed my son from Ismail. I cradled Khalil in my arms and offered him my breast, wanting him to believe I was not responsible for his pain. My relationship with my son had so far consisted of an unadulterated flow of love and nourishment. With this first betrayal, I planted our relationship firmly on this earth; in the soil of ambiguity and loss. My husband and the doctor tried to reassure me that the procedure had gone well, but I pushed right past them and fled the office with Khalil, imagining I could run fast enough to slip back into the past. My husband called out to me to wait for him at the elevator, but I was already halfway down the stairs.

Khalil fell into a deep sleep as soon as we pulled out of the parking lot, and we drove home in silence. Our son's foreskin was wrapped in a piece of gauze and tucked into Ismail's shirt pocket. I had been restless and angry on the way to the clinic, but now I felt raw, overwhelmed with grief and a crazy desire to somehow fold my baby back into my body. At home I curled around him in bed while my husband knelt beneath the young fig tree in our garden, said a prayer, and buried the foreskin in the earth.

Two years later, thumbing through a parenting magazine, I came across an article condemning circumcision. The author explained that by tickling both circumcised and uncircumcised infants on the penis and gauging the intensity of their laughter, scientists had determined that the circumcised penis is less sensitive than the uncircumcised one. I thought about how much I'd hated being tickled as a child, even as I'd laughed uncontrollably. I thought about my own sensitivities, which have brought me equal measures of joy and pain. I thought about the way my circumcised husband's face crumpled with pleasure during lovemaking and the warm tears I felt on his cheeks afterward. Could the quality of our sexual experiences really be reduced to the number of neurons that fire when our genitals are stimulated? Lovemaking, that morass of sensuality and spirit, didn't conform well to scientific research. But later that evening, after our children were in bed, I showed the article to Ismail. We sat out on our porch in silence, watching the night fall and cloak our home in shadows. After a while he told me he wished he had been able to listen to me better.

18 | *Liberation*

A few weeks before Gaddafi was captured and killed, I sat with Ismail on our back porch after the children had gone to bed. The plaster Buddha on the small stone table between us cradled a glowing tea candle in his lap. A bullfrog lowed from across the pond, and the cat at our feet hissed at an unseen threat in the woods.

"I cannot wait until Gaddafi is dead," Ismail said flatly, staring into the darkness.

I studied his tired eyes and the deep lines on his face. I covered his warm, heavy hand with my own.

"If Gaddafi were sitting as close to you as I am right now, close enough to touch—if you could look into his dull, disoriented eyes and his aging face—would you still wish him dead?" I asked. Ismail looked over at me briefly and then down again at the tabletop, fixing his eyes on the dying flame in the lap of the Buddha.

"If there is such a thing as pure hatred," he said, "it is what I feel toward Gaddafi."

Whenever I said I hated anything when I was a child, my mother winced and sharply drew in her breath. "Please don't hate," she would say, as if the word itself stung her flesh, and my sister and I would glance at one another and try not to laugh at her extreme sensitivity to the word. But once I saw the pure blank faces of my newborn children, their pristine gazes unblemished by darker human emotions, I understood how she felt. Even years later, after my children had grown moody and odorous and sullen, after I'd caught them lying or seen them disappear behind slamming doors, I still wanted to scrub the stains of darker human impulses from their skin. I pored over spirituality books and dreamed of a house that contained no rage or hate. Once, following a suggestion from one of these books, I announced that our house needed a peace room—a small, safe space to which any of us could retreat when the flames of our anger threatened to overtake the house. We did not have a room to spare, so instead I found a narrow space in the basement beneath the stairs, just high and wide enough for a child or grown-up to sit cross-legged beneath the underside of pine steps. I covered the cold tile floor with a blanket and a pillow and hung origami peace cranes from the floorboards overhead. I imagined making my way down the stairs the next time my husband raised his voice or pointed his finger at me; imagined the cranes gently tickling the top of his head as he sat cross-legged fuming over yet another library fine I had incurred. When my toddler daughter threw herself violently to the ground, as if her body were an outfit she wanted to cast off—when she screamed until her face was beet red and snot ran in rivulets from her nose—I gently suggested she take a little time for herself in the peace room. She never went willingly, so I had to carry her there, kicking and screaming. Her flailing arms sent origami paper cranes flying through the air. I had not realized how difficult my plan would be to implement. The peace room remained empty while anger erupted all over the house. Still, I clung to my vision of a family that resolved conflict peacefully and honored the humanity of others—even dictators of faraway countries.

I told Ismail that I hated to hear him sound so bloodthirsty and tribal. He reiterated his feelings about Gaddafi, this time raising his voice and pointing his finger at me. When I tried to respond, he cut me off. His voice grew louder; his finger jabbed at the air. Nothing would move him from the barren ground of his hatred. Ismail uttered an Arabic saying, then translated it for me: *It's a goat even if it has wings.* He meant to say he would not be moved from his position, no matter what—even, apparently, if all evidence pointed irrefutably to the fact that he was dead wrong. *Crazy Libyan*, I thought to myself as I got up and went inside.

Ismail bore the scars of oppression like an old and debilitating injury, one that would force him to walk off kilter for the rest of his life—even though he had lived in the United States long enough to recite his favorite lines from Oscar-winning movies and become more familiar with Bob Dylan's albums than I was. In college in Tripoli, he had listened to disco and smoked hashish and debated politics in dorm rooms. Then some students organized a political rally—and shortly afterward they disappeared. They were hung in the city's main square before students who were forced to watch, and their executions were broadcast repeatedly on state television. If he stayed in Libya, Ismail realized, he would end up dead or in jail. So when he won a scholarship overseas, he left his entire family behind, crushing all their expectations for a firstborn son. The guilt for having done so flared up in him like a virus, causing him to frequently plummet into brooding, defensive, and overly apologetic moods. He often awoke in the middle of the night in a cold sweat, fighting with tangled sheets and mumbling desperately in Arabic. He was deeply skeptical of male authority in general—and politicians in particular—and he exploded if any look or gesture made him feel censored in any way. He could no longer distinguish between self-restraint and suppression.

Gaddafi had encroached upon our marriage from the very beginning. On our first date, when we sat on a rooftop in downtown Chapel Hill watching the sun go down, my heart sank in disappointment when he told me his nationality. I had not been able to place his accent but had imagined that perhaps it was Spanish or Italian or even Moroccan. Each of those countries had its own romantic appeal; each lent itself easily to my fantasies. But Libya? It brought to mind a vague memory from my high school years: doing homework, I heard a television newscaster in the background announce that we had bombed a mad dictator in a decrepit, parched, terrorist-infested country called Libya—a nation that was so inconsequential, so obviously deserving of our attack and so incapable of retaliation, that this act didn't even warrant further discussion at the dinner table or mention in social studies class the next day.

Every hairpin turn, every dead end in Ismail's life could be traced back to Gaddafi. Even thousands of miles from his homeland, he still felt that no Libyan could be trusted, so he did not maintain a single friendship with one. He had only occasional contact with family, because when he called them, the so-called brother leader made his presence felt on phone lines. In stilted, one-sided conversations, relatives offered only curt, paranoid responses to his questions. When Ismail was a child, his illiterate father returned each evening from his small shop with a brown bag full of money, which had to be stretched to feed and support a family of ten. Then one day Gaddafi had announced that private businesses now belonged to the state. Everything my father-in-law had worked so hard to build and maintain slipped like minnows through his grasp, and he had tumbled into a despair as deep as the ocean that now separated him from his son. He grew more violent and withdrawn with each passing year, a brutal tyrant over his wife and children in the small home that was his only domain. The oppression that spread through Ismail's family was so pervasive and debilitating that I worried it would be passed on to our children like a hereditary disease.

I read that in his final days, Gaddafi was increasingly disoriented—lost without his buxom body guards and fawning servants, his audience of thousands trained to chant his praises on cue. Driven from his lavish palace to the dusty alleys of desert towns, whisked in darkness from house to abandoned house by his loyal driver and a few protectors, he survived on rice and water. Rumors abounded about his whereabouts: He had escaped Libya through a secret labyrinth of underground tunnels. He had booby-trapped the entire city of Tripoli. He had a diabolical plan to take all of his people to hell with him. He had tormented his people for so long they had come to see him as invincible; only an ending worthy of a Hollywood movie could bring him down. But instead he made the most primal and predictable choice of all: he fled back to his tribe in the desert, to the town where he had been born and raised.

It is said that he spent his last days reading the Qur'an. I try to imagine him cradling that holy book. Did he find solace in what he read? Not long after, bloody images of his broken body were broadcast to the entire world—but no video footage could show us what that book did to his heart, could reveal if it was broken wide open by what he found in its pages.

Dirty rats, he had called the rebels who ousted him, shaking his fist at the television cameras, promising to hunt them down alleys and flush them from sewers. In the end he was found huddled in a drainage pipe, caked in dirt and blood, driven out reeling and squinting into the brutal light. *Don't kill me, my sons.* He spread his arms wide, as if to embrace his attackers. In his final moments, when he fell to his knees and begged for his life, was he finally stripped of his illusions along with his torn and bloody clothes?

The day he died my family slid into the vinyl booth of a restaurant in a mini-mall near our house, beside a window that looked out onto the busy parking lot. My children sat across from me sipping soda from red plastic cups and studying the flat-screen television behind my head. Suddenly they froze, their matching brown eyes as wide as quarters, glued to the screen. I swiveled around to see Gaddafi's bloody face hovering over us on the muted television, begging for his life to the sound of the pop music that played on the jukebox. Then another image: rebels poking his bloody corpse on the ground with rifle butts. Ismail winced and turned away, horrified by the inhumanity of Gaddafi's final moments. "That's so wrong," he mumbled, shaking his head. "So wrong."

All around us, parents and children glanced up at the screen with bored expressions and mouths full of food. They watched while raising drinks to their lips or dipping corn chips into watery salsa. A new song came on the jukebox, a child spilled a glass of milk, a waitress wove through the room with a pitcher of margaritas. Gaddafi was not one of us, so we had no reason to be disturbed by the images on the screen. We knew right from wrong. We knew who was human, and deserving of our compassion, and who was less than that.

19 | *Surrender*

When Aliya was a newborn, I had danced her around our living room to the music of *Free to Be . . . You and Me,* the seventies children's classic whose every lyric about tolerance and gender equality I had memorized growing up in Southern California. Ismail sat with her for hours on our screened porch, swaying back and forth on a creaky metal rocker and singing old Arabic folk songs, and took her to a Muslim shaykh who chanted a prayer for long life into her tiny, velvety ear. Early on we'd decided we would raise her to choose what she identified with most from our dramatically different backgrounds.

I secretly felt smug about this agreement, confident that Aliya would favor my comfortable American lifestyle over Ismail's modest Muslim upbringing. My parents lived in a sprawling home in Santa Fe with a three-car garage, hundreds of channels on the flat-screen TV, organic food in the refrigerator, and a closetful of toys for the grandchildren. I imagined Aliya embracing shopping trips to Whole Foods and the stack

of presents under the Christmas tree while still fully appreci-
ating the melodic sound of Arabic, the honey-soaked baklava
Ismail made from scratch, the intricate henna tattoos her aunt
drew on her feet when we visited Libya.

The year she turned nine, we celebrated the end of Ramadan behind our local mosque. Children bounced in inflatable
fun houses while parents sat beneath a plastic tarp, shooing
flies from plates of curried chicken, golden rice, and baklava.
Aliya and I wandered past rows of vendors selling prayer mats,
henna tattoos, and Muslim clothing. When we reached a table
displaying head coverings, Aliya turned to me and pleaded,
"Please, Mom—can I have one?"

She riffled through neatly folded stacks of head scarves while
the vendor, an African American woman shrouded in black,
beamed at her. I had recently seen Aliya cast admiring glances
at Muslim girls her age. I quietly pitied them, covered in floor-
length skirts and long sleeves on even the hottest summer days,
as my best childhood memories were of my skin laid bare to
the sun: feeling the grass between my toes as I ran through
the sprinkler on my front lawn; wading into an icy river in
Idaho, my shorts hitched up my thighs, to catch my first rainbow trout; surfing an emerald wave off the coast of Hawaii. But
Aliya envied these girls and had asked me to buy clothes for her
like theirs. And now a head scarf.

In the past, my excuse was that they were hard to find at our
local mall, but here she was, offering to spend ten dollars from

her own allowance to buy the green rayon one she clutched in her hand. I started to shake my head emphatically *no* but caught myself, remembering my promise to Ismail. So I gritted my teeth and bought it.

That afternoon, as I was leaving for the grocery store, Aliya called out from her room that she wanted to come.

A moment later she appeared at the top of the stairs—or half of her did. From the waist down, she was my daughter: sneakers, jeans a little threadbare at the knees. But from the waist up, this girl was a stranger. Her bright, round face was suspended in a tent of dark cloth, like a moon in a starless sky.

"Are you going to wear that?" I asked.

"Yeah," she said slowly, in a tone she had recently begun to use with me when I stated the obvious.

On the way to the store, I stole glances at her in my rearview mirror. The same type of lightweight scarf that had seemed so comfortable and easy to wear in Libya felt far more oppressive here in my hometown, weighed down as it was by judgments and assumptions. Aliya stared out the window in silence, appearing as aloof and unconcerned as a Muslim dignitary visiting our small southern town—I, merely her chauffeur. I bit my lip. I wanted to ask her to remove her head covering before she got out of the car, but I couldn't think of a single logical reason why, except that the sight of it made my blood pressure rise. I'd always encouraged her to express her individuality and to resist peer pressure, but now I felt as self-conscious and claustrophobic as if I were wearing that head scarf myself.

In the Food Lion parking lot, the heavy summer air smothered my skin. I gathered the damp hair on my neck into a ponytail, but Aliya seemed unfazed by the heat. We must have looked like an odd pair: a tall blonde woman in a tank top and jeans cupping the hand of a four-foot-tall Muslim. I drew my daughter closer and the skin on my bare arms prickled—as much from protective instinct as from the blast of refrigerated air that hit me as I entered the store.

As we maneuvered our cart down the aisles, shoppers glanced at us like a riddle they couldn't quite solve, quickly dropping their gaze when I caught their eye. In the produce aisle, a woman reaching for an apple fixed me with an overly bright, solicitous smile that said, *I embrace diversity and I am perfectly fine with your child.* At the checkout line, an elderly southern woman clasped her bony hands together and bent slowly down toward Aliya. "My, my," she drawled, wobbling her head in disbelief. "Don't you look absolutely precious!" My daughter smiled politely, then turned to ask me for a pack of gum.

In the following days, Aliya wore her head scarf to the breakfast table over her pajamas, to a Muslim gathering where she was showered with compliments, and to the park, where the moms with whom I chatted studiously avoided mentioning it altogether.

Later that week, at our local pool, I watched a girl only a few years older than Aliya play Ping-Pong with a boy her age. She was caught in that awkward territory between childhood and adolescence—narrow hips, skinny legs, the slightest swelling of new breasts—and she wore a bikini. Her opponent wore an oversized T-shirt and baggy trunks that fell below his knees, and when he slammed the ball at her, she lunged for it while trying with one hand to keep the slippery strips of spandex in place. I wanted to offer her a towel to wrap around her hips, so she could lose herself in the contest and feel the exhilaration of making a perfect shot. It was easy to see why she was getting demolished at this game: Her near-naked body was consuming her focus. And in her pained expression I recognized the familiar mix of shame and excitement I felt when I first wore a bikini.

At fourteen, I'd skittered down the halls of high school like a squirrel in traffic: hugging the walls, changing direction in midstream, darting for cover. Then I went to Los Angeles to visit my aunt Mary during winter break. Mary collected mermaids, kept a black-and-white photo of her long-haired Indian guru on her dresser, and shopped at a tiny health food store that smelled of patchouli and peanut butter. She took me to Venice Beach, where I bought a cheap bikini from a street vendor.

Dizzy with the promise of my own bikini, I thought I could be someone else—glistening and proud like the greased-up bodybuilders on the lawn, relaxed and unself-conscious as the hippies who lounged on the pavement with lit incense tucked behind their ears. In a beachside bathroom with gritty cement floors, I changed into my new two-piece suit.

Goose bumps spread across my chubby white tummy and

the downy white hairs on my thighs stood on end—I felt as raw and exposed as a turtle stripped of its shell. And when I left the bathroom, the stares of men seemed to pin me in one spot even as I walked by.

In spite of a strange and mounting sense of shame, I was riveted by their smirking faces; in their suggestive expressions I thought I glimpsed some vital clue to the mystery of myself. What did these men see in me—what was this strange power surging between us, this rapidly shifting current that one moment made me feel powerful and the next unspeakably vulnerable?

Now I imagined Aliya in a bikini in only a few years. Then I imagined her draped in Muslim attire. It was hard to say which image was more unsettling. I thought then of something a Sufi Muslim friend had told me: that Sufis believe that our essence radiates beyond our physical bodies—that we have a sort of energetic second skin, which is extremely sensitive and permeable to everyone we encounter. Muslim men and women wear modest clothing, she said, to protect this charged space between themselves and the world.

Growing up in Southern California, I had learned that freedom for women meant, among other things, fewer clothes, and that women could be anything—and still look good in a bikini. My physical freedom had been an important part of my process of self-discovery, but the exposure had come at a price.

Since that day in Venice Beach, I'd spent years learning to

swim in the turbulent currents of physical attraction—wanting to be desired, resisting others' unwelcome advances, plumbing the mysterious depths of my own longing. I'd spent countless hours studying my reflection in the mirror—admiring it, hating it, wondering what others thought of it. It seemed to me that if I had applied the same relentless scrutiny to another subject I could have become enlightened, completed a doctorate degree, or at least figured out how to grow an organic vegetable garden.

One afternoon I tried on designer jeans in the crowded dressing room of a large department store, alongside college girls in stiletto heels, young mothers with babies fussing in their strollers, and middle-aged women with glossed lips pursed into frowns. One by one we filed into changing rooms, then lined up to take our turns on a brightly lit pedestal surrounded by mirrors, cocking our hips, sucking in our tummies, and craning our necks to stare at our rear ends. When it was my turn, my heart felt as tight in my chest as my legs did in the jeans. My face looked drawn under the fluorescent lights. Suddenly I was exhausted by all the years I'd spent doggedly chasing the carrot of self-improvement, while dragging behind me a heavy cart of self-criticism.

Aliya at nine was captivated by the world around her—not by what she saw in the mirror. The previous summer she stood at the edge of the Blue Ridge Parkway, stared at the blue-black outline of the mountains in the distance, their tips swaddled by cottony clouds, and gasped. "This is the most beautiful thing I ever saw," she whispered. Her wide-open eyes were a mirror for all that beauty, and she stood so still that she blended into the lush landscape, until finally we broke her reverie by pulling her back to the car.

But in her fourth-grade class, girls were already drawing a connection between clothing and popularity. A few weeks ago, she'd told me angrily about a classmate who had ranked all the girls in class according to how stylish they were. That's when I realized that while physical exposure had liberated me in some ways, Aliya might discover an entirely different type of freedom by choosing to cover herself.

One morning when I dropped her off at school, instead of driving away from the curb in a rush as I usually did, I watched her walk into a crowd of kids, bent forward under the weight of her backpack as if she were bracing against a storm. She moved purposefully, in such a solitary way—so different from the way I was at her age, and I realized once again how mysterious she was to me. It wasn't just her head covering. It was her lack of concern for what others thought about her. It was finding her stash of Halloween candy untouched in her drawer in the middle of spring, whereas I'd been a child obsessed with sweets. It was the fact that she would rather dive into a book than into the ocean, that she could be so consumed with her reading that she wouldn't hear me calling her from the next room.

I watched her kneel at the entryway to her school and pull a neatly folded cloth from the front of her pack. Then she slipped it over her head, and her shoulders disappeared beneath it like the cape her younger brother wore when he pretended to be a superhero.

As I pulled away from the curb, I imagined that head scarf having magical powers to protect her boundless imagination, her keen perception, and her unself-conscious goodness. I imagined it shielding her on her journey through adolescence, that house of mirrors where so many young women get trapped. I imagined the scarf buffering her from the restlessness and insecurity that clings to us in spite of the growing number of choices at our fingertips; I imagined it providing safe cover as she took flight into a future I could only imagine.

THE SUMMER I turned thirteen, when my parents thought I was playing kick the can in the street as dusk hovered over the New Mexico mountains, I was actually in the dark corner of my neighbor's garage, watching nervously as he reached behind his father's heavy metal toolbox and pulled out a *Hustler* magazine. We sat cross-legged on the concrete floor, he spread the centerfold across his lap, and together we studied the strangest woman I had ever seen. Her mysterious expression was at once startled and inviting: arched eyebrows, wide hungry eyes, the slight upward curl of a lip. To me the most disconcerting aspect of her was that she seemed comfortable—even playful—in the most minimal and embarrassing of clothing and the most shameless of poses.

My neighbor sighed, squinting and shoving his glasses up his nose with one thumb to get a better look; he was hypnotized. But this image had the opposite effect on me: I squirmed with a keen and painful awareness of my awkward body on the cold concrete. Most evenings that summer we'd met on the corner to play touch football in the street or explore the canyons behind our houses. We had similar tastes in sports, fantasy novels, even clothing: faded cutoffs with ragged edges, loose cotton T-shirts, and tennis shoes. Now, crouched beside him studying this picture, I suddenly noticed my chubby thighs, the downy hair on my shins, the high collar of my boxy T-shirt. I drew my knees to my chest, as mortified as if the nakedness on the page were my own. What men wanted, I realized in an instant, was the opposite of me: women who were arched and silken as cats, splayed out and submissive.

Sexuality, it seemed to me then and for many years afterward, was for women a form of theater—a rigorous, carefully choreographed performance for an audience of one. Though she always played the starring role, the woman never chose her own lines or costume. My biggest obstacle to a successful performance was a stubborn, deep-seated streak of modesty—a paralyzing reluctance to put myself on display. To be as limp and flawless as a porcelain doll, as malleable as a marionette, went against every instinct I had. More than one teenage boy, in a moment of groping exasperation, implored me to stop being so "uptight." I couldn't help it.

My freshman year in college, I moved into a Southern

California dormitory perched on the cliffs over what I had no idea was a nude beach. The first time I jogged down the steep trail to the shoreline, I was shocked to discover so many naked men strolling across the sand or sitting spread-eagled staring out at the horizon, their dangling pink parts cooking like sausages in the sun. I learned to lock my eyes on the packed sand at the edge of the surf as I ran, to absorb myself in the bubbling sea foam, and to never stop to catch my breath—because the moment I did, one of the naked men would approach me without fail to ask me the time of day. Around this time I joined a nature club for students like me who loved outdoor adventures. The club was full of robust, androgynous undergrads: men with glossy blond ponytails and flannel shirts tied like skirts around narrow waists; women with muscled arms and furry legs. One hot afternoon we hiked in the desert, and as the sun bore down on us, my companions began to peel off their shirts one by one—first the men and then, wordlessly, the women, too. In the end I was the only one left wearing a cotton T-shirt soaked through with nervous perspiration.

Discovering feminist literature my first year in college only added to my confusion. Authors I admired gave me powerful messages that I was free to express myself sexually; failing to do so, in fact, would be unhealthy and wrong, a sign of patriarchal oppression. But here on the Southern California coast, the western capital of physical perfection, there was a catch. My so-called sexual freedom must meet certain unspoken criteria:

high swollen breasts and a flat, tanned belly, silky lingerie and hairless thighs skinny enough to always allow a sliver of light to pass between them. Sex itself could look like hundreds of different positions, as long as I remained in character: innocent yet brazen, devoted yet undemanding, petulant yet submissive. Layered and contradictory, it was nearly an impossible role to play. I sweated like a Shakespearean actor weighed down by a heavy costume and cumbersome couplets, too anxious for applause to ever really enjoy myself.

In truth, my desires were nothing like images I saw on the screen or in magazines. There was nothing theatrical about my preferences: loving touches beneath a veil of darkness, warm skin and soft cotton sheets. I never liked lingerie. I had no fantasies about whips or leather, no made-up stories to act out in costume. I never imagined skin pounding and colliding. Instead my erotic mind was a mosaic of image and sensation: a blooming night flower with a moist, delicate center. A spoonful of honey fed into a hungry mouth. A garden washed by the merciful rain, dew on a petal like sweat pearling on flesh. *Tell me your fantasy,* my boyfriend whispered to me in the dark. Propped up on one arm, he studied my face, eagerly waiting for me to turn him on. The silence stretched out; I had nothing to say. My deepest longing had no characters, setting, or narrative arc. My most erotic fantasy was simply that I was enough: plain, holy, beautiful.

. . .

THE FIRST TIME my skin touched Ismail's, we were standing in his kitchen, two glasses of cold water on the counter between us. We had just finished a run; we were flushed and smiling. He placed his hand gently over mine, and the unexpected heat from his palm sent a jolt of electricity up my arm. I nearly jumped, hypervigilant about what his next move might be. It was a familiar and nerve-racking feeling, this heightened alertness in response to a man's unexpected pass. I had known men who scrambled toward sex like racing toward a finish line. But Ismail did nothing else but hold my gaze and smile while his hand rested over mine. I couldn't help but smile, too, and silence stretched out as I investigated the sensation of his skin. Not since I was fourteen, and the boy seated beside me at church reached for my hand and held it through the sermon, could I recall ever having been given so much time to investigate such a small pleasure.

I soon discovered that Ismail relished small intimacies: holding my gaze, sweeping a strand of hair from my face, prolonging a doorway embrace when we said good-bye. Dropping me off at my house at the end of an evening, he reminded me of a teenage boy: awkwardly extending the conversation in the dark, reaching over the center console to find my hand, leaning across the emergency brake for a hesitant kiss. He moved at an entirely different pace from other men I had known—as if sex were not the grand prize, as if each connection were a revelation. I figured this must have come from spending his teens and twenties in a Muslim country where sex was strictly prohibited, where fleeting stolen intimacies were all a young man could hope for.

A MODERN, LIBERATED American woman is only supposed to practice submission when toys, costumes, or accessories are involved. In the theater of sexuality we are given a pass, allowed to leave our political correctness at the door. In any other aspect of our lives, submission is seen as weakness. When I moved to North Carolina to attend graduate school, southern summers taught me my first lesson in surrender. On a sweltering July day, I moved into a tiny green house on the edge of a meadow whose overgrown grass stood utterly still in the hot clotted air. The unwieldy air-conditioning unit propped in my bedroom window groaned day and night, delivering a weak stream of relief that evaporated like steam from a kettle. Never one to nap in California, I fell asleep in the middle of the day on my living room futon, awaking to discover my body seeping a shadowy imprint onto its cotton cover. I had to escape the dark oven of this house; I was melting into the furniture. I swung open the door and collided with a wall of hot, thick air.

That first month I stumbled around town muttering like a madwoman, dripping sweat and fuming with resentment for the infernal humidity. I once heard a southerner describe summer days like these as close: *The weather was close.* It was true: the wet heat wrapped me in its moist, fleshy arms, smothered me against its sticky bosom, and refused to let go. Southern summer afternoons climbed onto my lap like a big, hairy dog, its hot breath in my face. I took its assault personally: for three months I was offended on a daily basis by its impositions, outraged by its relentless assault. But over time I learned to submit to the season. I discovered the wisdom of rocking chairs on screened porches, tall glasses of sweet tea, early morning runs in the woods and lazy afternoons at the pool. I rediscovered the pleasure of finishing thick novels. I learned to yield to the season, to find what was good and be grateful for it.

Marriage taught me my second lesson in surrender: I learned to submit to my beloved like a mother submits to an infant's hunger, offering an aching swollen breast and feeling the sweet relief of doing exactly what she was meant to do. On a good night, when there was peace between us and neither one fell into bed exhausted, Ismail reached for me with gentle, insistent hands. I practiced molding my form to his: my body poised and quivering, tuned by his undivided attention, ready to be played like an instrument. His touch softened my flesh like butter. My body rose to meet his; my skin yielded gratefully to his pressure. Under love's blanket, there was nothing theatrical or passive about my surrender. It was assertive, ecstatic, playful. He was trained on my pleasure, which then became his own. Giving and receiving became one, as indivisible as a body and a soul.

"How would you rate your love life?" he whispered into my left ear. I was curled on my side, staring out the window at the bright, unblinking moon. His arms around me were soft as worn cotton.

How could I possibly place this love on a scale? If ten was the ecstatic fusion of divine love, the white-hot annihilation of the small separate self, and one was the loneliness and despair of the wrong marriage, then all the years of our married life I had played this scale like a piano, my fingers dancing over all the keys, using each note to make haunting, beautiful music.

"I would not rate it," I murmured and then, nudging him with my heel in a reprimand, added, "That would not be a very Muslim thing to do, would it?"

He pulled me closer, tucked his chin into the small depression of my clavicle, his face so close that I could hear the nearly inaudible pop of his parting lips: the sound of him smiling in the dark.

"*Alhamdu lillah* is my answer to your question," I whispered. "*Alhamdu lillah.*"

All praise is due to God.

Quiet for a moment, he contemplated my response. And then, propping himself up on one elbow so he could see me: "How exactly would you say it?"

He wanted to study my face as I spoke the word, to discover if I said it with a teasing smile and laughter in my eyes. Did I say it earnestly, with humble gratitude for a gift so precious it warranted no other word? Or did I say the word with a distant look in my eye and a long, forbearing sigh, as one enduring a difficult trial?

These were important distinctions. The straightforward translation for *Alhamdu lillah* is "all praise belongs to God," but the way it is expressed creates nuanced differences in meaning. It is a heavy, solid container of a phrase—deep enough to hold self-pity, complacency, gratitude or awe. Sometimes when I ask a Muslim friend how she is doing, she replies with a long sigh, and her *Alhamdu lillah* tells me she is struggling to be patient and find blessing in difficulty. Spoken with a certain grim determination, it can mean "if God's plan is for me to endure this tribulation, then I accept it." At other times the word is awash with humility, each syllable pouring forth gratitude like water over river stones. No matter how it is spoken, the word washes away our small self-referential stories about the vast mystery of our lives. Trying to find its secular English equivalent, Ismail sometimes responds to the question "How are you?" by saying "I can't complain." But this phrase is a poor substitute, the domineering *I* pushing God out altogether and colonizing meaning, forcing each word that follows to march in single file behind the self. *Alhamdu lillah* wipes away the self altogether, like the swipe of an eraser against a chalkboard on which our most cherished stories are written. I murmured the word again, smiling in the dark.

20 | Prayer

The last time he went to Libya, Ismail purchased six prayer rugs in Tripoli's Old City. The night he arrived home, he hauled his suitcase into our living room, unzipped the bag, and spread the rugs across the floor: six different border designs, six different shades of minarets and tassels. The rugs smelled faintly of incense and dust and the rusty roll-down doors that shopkeepers bring clattering to the ground at the end of a market day.

I was grateful to finally have my own set; prayer rugs were as essential to a Muslim gathering as a nice set of wineglasses were to a cocktail party. In the past I had felt sheepish when a Muslim guest peered out the window at the fading light, checked her watch, and asked if she could borrow a prayer rug to pray. Offering her a towel or a folded blanket was as wrong as serving good wine in a paper cup. Now I imagined passing out my six prayer rugs one by one, to three couples—or maybe two couples and two single people who might enjoy meeting one another. Watching my guests line them up side by side on the carpet, I'd feel the holy satisfaction of anticipating a guest's every need.

The next time we invited Muslim friends for a gathering, thirty people came. When it was time to pray, we moved aside furniture in our living room to make space for two rows of prayer rugs. Some guests had brought their own; others used ours. Lined up side by side, the rugs made a colorful mosaic of minarets on which our guests rose and fell in unison, *Allahu Akhbar* pulsing through the room like a single heartbeat. Afterward the rugs were refolded and stacked by the door for our friends to reclaim on their way out. At the end of the evening I walked each guest to the threshold, gave away neatly packaged leftovers, thanked them for coming, and said "Peace be with you" as they put on their shoes. I kissed the women on each cheek, touched the faces of the children, and put my hand over my heart as I said good-bye to the men, holding their gaze just long enough for them to see the love and gratitude in my eyes. After closing the door behind the last guest, I went to put away my prayer rugs.

There were only five. One was missing.

"One of our prayer rugs is missing," I announced, standing in the doorway to the kitchen and addressing Ismail's back. He was at the sink, rinsing water glasses and loading them into the dishwasher.

"I'm sure it will turn up," he murmured, without turning to

look at me. I went back through my stack, then swept through the living room. Nothing.

"It's definitely not here." I reclaimed my place in the doorway and crossed my arms over my chest. Ismail shrugged, a noncommittal gesture that said, *No big deal* or *It's not my fault.* Either way, I found it annoying.

I could not stop thinking about my missing prayer rug. I imagined it folded at a friend's house, someone else snapping it open and lying it across the floor for *her* guest. I mentioned it to a friend who said she might have ended up with an extra one. I breathed a sigh of relief—but then she asked me to please describe my missing rug so she could verify I was the rightful owner. This test I did not expect. I could not recall its color or pattern. I knew it only as rug number six. I smiled politely and changed the subject, but my stomach clenched with anger. She had my rug. I knew it.

Later, when I asked Ismail to describe the missing rug to me, he told me he would recognize it if he saw it. As far as I could see, there was only one way to solve this mystery: Ismail and I would drop in to visit friends during prayer times. Each day Muslims were required to pray five times, and each of the five prayers had its own name: Fajr, Zuhr, Asr, Maghrib, and Isha. The first and the last prayer of the day fell outside of acceptable visiting hours—I could think of no good excuse to show up at someone's house just as the first sliver of light appeared in the dawn sky or right before they went to bed—and another prayer fell in the middle of the workday. That left us with two options: the late-afternoon prayer, Asr, and the early-evening prayer, Maghrib. I figured we could kill two birds with one stone by dropping in on friends who lived farther away during Asr. We might show up just as they were unloading groceries or chopping up vegetables for dinner. We would chat for a while, and then Ismail would look down at his watch. "Shall we pray?" he would ask—a question that left room for only one answer. He would discreetly inspect the rugs as they were laid out. If he did not see ours, we would still have time to graciously excuse ourselves and hit another friend's house by Maghrib.

When I described my plan to my husband, he studied my face for a long moment. Then he shook his head slowly.

"No way," he said. "If something else were missing from our house, I'd help you track it down—but not a prayer rug. You're just going to have to be at peace with the fact that someone is touching their forehead to it in prayer."

SPRING ARRIVED WITH an explosion of green. In our new house, it was my first season of tending plants whose names I was still learning: camellia, jasmine, forsythia. A gardener friend told me I needed to cut my butterfly bushes down to the ground. Only when the plant was relieved of the burden of last year's fading leaves, she explained, would it explode with new growth. Same went for the rosebush. She was a master gardener, so I should have trusted her, but I was skeptical. I was attached to the tangled branches that lined my walkway to the back porch, concealing an electric box and plain siding behind purple flowers and green foliage. I didn't like the idea of losing all that fullness; I worried about the empty space that would be exposed by such aggressive pruning. What if the plants never grew back as high and lush as they now were? To hack away so much of a living thing felt violent, so instead I trimmed hesitantly, taking too little to make a noticeable difference.

But as I worked I couldn't help but notice the brittleness of the branches, the dullness of once vibrant leaves, the desiccated brown remnants of purple blooms. Tiny green shoots near the ground, fresh and new, ignited my imagination, and I began to wonder what else might emerge from the dark soil if I cleared away the half-dead remnants of the past. So the following day, armed with my husband's gloves and a pair of shears, I attacked the bush. I slashed at the undergrowth, forced my way through branches as thick as my thumb, brittle on the outside but still sinewy with life at the center. I cut and cleared, pulled at dead limbs, my elation growing along with the pile of branches beside me. Hacking away at the faded aftermath of a bygone season, I thought, *This is my life, a tangle of half-dead relationships and routines, diminishing pleasures, faded habits, and brittle assumptions*. I felt myself fading, felt the enervation of sustaining half-dead branches of myself. And yet I'd been afraid to cut it away, to confront the emptiness, afraid of what might grow from emptiness and whether it would be lush enough to satisfy me.

SOMETHING INSIDE ME was withering. I was not addicted to alcohol or drugs. I never lost a job or destroyed a marriage or racked up a mountain of debt from gambling. I was going to work every day, stopping by the grocery store on the way home, keeping the house tidy and exercising regularly and helping my kids with their homework and returning emails and phone calls. I was bottoming out quietly in that stylish suburban middle-class American way: my life not shattered by a single explosive addiction but slowly strangled in the web of so many small ones. Like a grasshopper who has taken a leap into an invisible web—its trembling limbs announcing its arrival to the spider that skitters closer to weave a gossamer shroud. No longer the brilliant green leaping creature he once was, his once-strong legs now paralyzed, his big black eyes now hidden behind a film of gray.

At night I slept restlessly, the chime of my husband's iPhone announcing the arrival of emails at regular intervals throughout the night from China and India and Europe, inquiries flagged with a red exclamation mark from corporate clients whose gushing cash flow had briefly been obstructed by a glitch in the software. In restless dreams, money was my oxygen, fed into my old and withered nostrils at the end of my life. I woke early in the morning, rose like a zombie from bed, and stumbled downstairs, summoned by the call to prayer of two lords: caffeine and the Internet. I ground coffee, set the kettle to boil, and logged on to the computer. Now my face was lit up by the dim glow of email and Facebook. The blank slate of my rested mind quickly grew cluttered with pictures of my high school boyfriend's Hawaiian vacation, stills from YouTube videos, close-up shots of the meals distant acquaintances had eaten the night before. One friend I had never met posted cholesterol levels from yesterday's physical exam; another posted a picture of her toddler on the toilet. Now my fingers were tapping, my mind was racing, the kettle was shrieking, the holy silence was evaporating. Here was a video of a talking shell that kept a dust mite for a pet, here was another of a white-bearded Sufi in Pakistan, here was one more of a motivational speaker whose talk about overcoming anxiety had gotten seven hundred thousand hits. I was listening to Bob Dylan, to a stand-up comedy routine, to the silence of a giraffe giving birth, to the thud of her baby falling from her womb onto to the cold, hard ground. I was racing around the world, and I was nowhere.

COME HERE, ISMAIL said. *Sit down.* He was in the living room. I was in the kitchen putting away the last of the dishes. *Just a second.* One more spoon to return to a drawer. One more quick wipe of the countertop. One more stack of papers to sort through and walk out to the recycling bin.

Please, come.

I sighed, put down what I was doing, and went and sat down across from him in the living room. The kids were in bed; the house rested under a blanket of silence. Ismail stared down at the Qur'an on his lap, took a deep breath, and began to recite. *Bismillah ar rahman ir rahim*—"in the name of God, the most compassionate, the most merciful." His was the voice of a stranger, high and pleading. I closed my eyes and listened to the strange sound—not exactly singing or chanting but something else altogether.

Over the years I had heard the Qur'an recited only a few times before, and each time it had gotten under my skin: the sound of a human voice saturated with longing, calling out to the unseen. The first time I heard it, I recoiled like I had accidentally stumbled upon someone naked; the sound was so vulnerable it made me want to turn and flee. But when I bore witness to that expression, it broke my calcified heart wide open, releasing the floodwater of compassion usually contained by the high dam of my ego.

One night, at a Muslim banquet, I was seated in a hotel's cavernous banquet room, at a table covered with platters of hummous and pita, halal chicken and tall glasses of iced tea. When I entered the banquet hall I had scanned that crowded room in search of a single person I might relate to, instantly discounting all those brightly covered feminine heads, women who looked to me like they belonged not just in a faraway country but in a distant century. I dismissed, too, all those dark-skinned Muslim men in their pressed slacks and buttoned-up shirts, their dark hair combed or concealed beneath skull caps, grown men who looked so neat and earnest it was as if their mothers had dressed them. I sighed. I had reluctantly agreed to come to this gathering with Ismail, expecting it would be exactly like this: no one for me to talk to, no one to giggle with me or pass the time. I smiled politely at the strangers seated around me at the banquet table, then stared down at the blank canvas of the tablecloth, rolling the ice from my water glass across my tongue and wishing it was wine. I looked surreptitiously at my watch, mentally calculating what time we'd be home and whether I would make it in time for my favorite television show.

A man from the local mosque began the program by standing at the podium to welcome everyone. His short speech was peppered with references to God as if he were the honored guest this evening. Praise be to God for the crowd gathered here tonight, and God willing we would enjoy this fine program, and in the name of God let's listen to a recitation from the Qur'an. He stepped aside and a skinny young man strode across the stage, nearly disappearing behind the podium. Silence fell as his lips moved in silent prayer, to the hum of air-conditioning and the *clink* of silverware against porcelain. Then he took a deep breath and began to recite, and it was as if an invisible hand turned down the volume of my internal chatter while turning up the volume on his plaintive, androgynous voice. Sharp as a surgeon's knife, this sound pierced me to the quick before I realized what was happening. Tears streamed down my cheeks; the rhythm and rhyme of his words were a turning of the knife. I felt as if I had been wandering in a desert, and his voice was water. I was parched for this sound. I gulped it in—but drinking was not enough. I wanted to pour it over my head, dive deep beneath its surface, try to touch the very bottom of this melody.

As he held the last note of his recitation, his Adam's apple bobbed on his skinny neck like it was trying to break free—and then it was over. The sound stopped abruptly, and I came up sputtering for air. The lanky, acne-faced man at the podium bore no resemblance to the vibration that had filled the room. Looking around me, I saw a few other shining faces that told me they, too, had been drinking in this music, that we had been swimming together in the same ocean. The moment passed. A silver-haired academic took his place behind the podium and began to speak about the immigrant Muslim experience, his catalog of facts and ironclad logic like so many links in a chain locking me back into my intellectual mind after my brief foray into my boundless heart. By the time his speech was over, the recitation was a half-remembered dream. I didn't even speak to Ismail about it on the way home.

I did not hear the Qur'an recited again until a couple of years later. One night Ismail told me about a famous reciter whose plaintive voice had been the background sound track of his youth. He found a video online and invited me to sit with him and listen. On the tiny screen, a bald old man with shining obsidian eyes began to make this noise from deep in his being—somewhere between a wail and a song, somewhere between a harmony and a howl. Tears streamed down his face as he sang, as if God were wringing him out like a washcloth. He wiped his wrinkled face in a steady motion as he continued to recite, his graceful fingers caressing his cheeks the entire time he was making this otherworldly sound, as if his hands were no longer his own, but the hands of Allah, laid upon him to grant the gift of this haunting music.

Yet in all our years together, I had never heard Ismail recite. How strange it is, the way two people who have shared a bed for over a decade can stumble into awkward new intimacy, can discover secrets between them after so many years. He closed his eyes. The voice that filled the room came from a stranger. Not the man who grumbled about the headlines each morning. Not the man who ran for an hour, then sat on our back porch peeling off his sweat-soaked socks. Not the man whose iPhone buzzed at his hip like a living thing. Not the man who turned up the music and danced with his children on weekend nights. This pure, plaintive voice was the sound of a child in a Libyan madrassah: a lanky, earnest boy who stayed up late practicing his Qur'anic recitation by the dim light of a kerosene lamp, refusing to blow it out and rest until the words were perfect. The boy who shot out of the madrassah at the end of his school day and ran to the souk, where he knew his illiterate and volatile father waited impatiently for him to record the day's transactions in the heavy, ink-smeared ledger. But in that moment in the madrassah, when he recited the Qur'an, he was able to briefly forget everything else but this. His eyelids fell like velvet curtains, and the words spilled from his lips as naturally as if they were his own—they became his own—filled with the longing of his own heart. My focus had been shattered into a million pieces, but like mercury to a magnet, his voice drew me in, gathered up my splintered spirit and made me whole again.

OMAR STOOD ON my doorstep, smiling and peering at me through square, outdated glasses. He placed his hand over his heart in a traditional Muslim greeting and stepped inside. His disabled son shuffled in, too, with a mischievous smile, as if the joke were on us, dragging half his body behind him like heavy luggage. A friend of Ismail's, Omar had lived all over the world but moved to our hometown to care for his elderly father, whom he visited each evening in a nursing home. That afternoon he sat cross-legged on our living room floor in pressed pants and a collared shirt, drinking tea and having a passionate conversation with my husband about politics, social justice, and Islam.

The news headlines often link Islam and violence, but Omar was one of the most peaceful people I had ever met. I wanted to know what made him so humble and patient, what inspired him to care so deeply for the oppressed and take such good care of his family and, when I asked him how he was doing, to respond with a smiling *"Alhamdu lillah"*—as if every bit of it were a blessing.

So when he sent me a one-line email—"For anyone on a spiritual path, this is a must-see"—I clicked the link. A grainy video transported me to a windowless room where dark-skinned men were crowded shoulder to shoulder in cheap plastic chairs. A bearded man stood before them: intense, near-black eyes, his head swaddled in a white turban. This was no prestigious university or Western conference center; this was the stuff of American nightmares: a poor, dark, faraway place where violent, irrational men plot our downfall. Why was Omar sending me this?

If the major world religions were schoolchildren, Islam would be the outcast. Buddhism, Judaism, and Christianity would roam the playground together, swinging from the monkey bars and making up games and resolving their own disputes. Hinduism would be more solitary—flamboyant and misunderstood. Islam would be the troubled one, mired in conflict, battling a reputation that preceded it.

It's surprising, since Islam is really so much like the other Abrahamic faiths: touched by sexism from the get-go, adapted to various cultures along the way, open to a range of interpretations, marred by violence and eternally in dispute. But the living heart of Islam is beautiful and pure.

The Shaykh on the video began to speak. Was that a

California accent? It was! I leaned in to listen and he reminded me that I would not find happiness in status or possessions, that I must take my fleeting life seriously. "Every breath takes you one breath closer to your final destination." Like a splash of cold water to my face, his words startled me awake from vivid dreams of vanity and immortality. He taught that this body I cherished and adorned was a just a temporary home for my spirit, which would one day fly away like a bird released from its cage. Stripped to its essentials, his message sounded like the dharma teachings at the Buddhist temple where I sometimes went to meditate.

I'D BEEN MARRIED to a Muslim for twelve years, but I'd never explored the faith—nor did Ismail pressure me to. According to Islam, he explained, every people have their own prophet; many paths lead to God. So he kept to his prayers, and I kept to my morning meditation. Each day during the month of Ramadan I prepared a plate of dates for him at dusk so he could break his fast, and each December he sorted through our photos to help me select one for the family Christmas card. But mostly we steered clear of one another's baffling rituals.

Buddhism had been part of my life since college, when I'd stumbled across Charlotte Joko Beck's illuminating text *Every-day Zen*. But there were two words I tripped over, syllables like boulders blocking my path forward: nothingness and empti-ness. No matter how many years I spent counting my breath or naming my thoughts, I could not bring myself closer to that abyss Buddhism said was the center of my life.

Maybe that's partly why I was drawn to this American Muslim teacher who taught that at the heart of our existence was infinite mercy and divine unity. "Meaning is everywhere," he preached. "May God open our hearts to the meaning of our existence." I was struck by the love I heard in his voice and by the way he wove God into every other sentence. In the nominally Christian household of my childhood, I'd been taught never to take God's name in vain; *Jesus Christ* was an epithet reserved for moments of great exasperation. In Islam no circumstance was too trivial, intimate, or explosive to warrant invoking God's name.

Fervent spiritual seekers once made long, treacherous journeys to study with the great masters. Today even halfhearted seekers with ADD can find them: the best teachers of every tradition are just a mouse click away. I downloaded the Shaykh's teachings, originally delivered to audiences in Canada, Europe, the Middle East, and Africa. At dawn, as I jogged along a dirt trail beside the creek, he spoke of a merciful God. He explained that the Arabic word for mercy—*rahma*—came from the Arabic word for womb, and that women had a spiritual advantage over men. "Humanity's best qualities are found naturally in women, but must be acquired by men," he taught. He went on to say that, like Christians, Muslims honored Mary as the mother of Jesus but that in Islam, Jesus was also honored because he was her son. Muslims revered her; many scholars believed she had the stature of a prophet, and she was referenced more often in the Qur'an than in the Bible. I did not expect a Muslim teacher to speak so reverently about women—or to refer so eloquently to great Western literature. He cited Shakespeare and Yeats alongside ancient Muslim teachers, and he spoke with insight about the human condition. "To validate our own pain, we deny the pain of others," he said. "But only in acknowledging others' pain can we achieve our full humanity."

He was an American convert, and his idealism and intensity reminded me of my college friend, a wild-eyed philosopher who burned with passion to know God, save the world, and do something extraordinary with his brief and precious life. But unlike my old friend, whose insights were dulled by alcohol or marijuana, the Shaykh's intellect was razor sharp. His mind and heart were engaged at full throttle and in perfect balance, like the twin engines that lift a massive jet improbably toward the heavens.

"What's the name of that guy you're into? Osama Sultana?" a friend asked, and the others giggled. We were seated around a fire pit in my backyard on a cool spring evening. I'd recently told her the name of the Muslim teacher whose lectures had moved me so deeply. The Arabic syllables had swirled in her imagination with billowing black smoke, *Arabian Nights,* tumbling towers, a fine-featured man with coffee-colored skin in a mountaintop cave. *Osama Sultana.*

One girlfriend had just completed a triathlon, another was starting her own company, and a third had just returned from a business trip to Europe. They were smart, funny, and adventurous, willing to explore any subject in conversation—except for God. Even my friend who took her twins to Sunday school studiously avoided the subject—as if she visited him only once a week in the sprawling church off the freeway where he lived, that impressive estate that floated in a sea of SUVs and minivans on Sunday mornings.

When I told my girlfriends the Shaykh reminded me of a prophet, they flashed one another warning looks. They'd much rather talk about controversial subjects like polyamory or pot legalization than prophets.

"Like Martin Luther King reminds me of a prophet," I hastened to add, to show I was no zealot. Devout Muslims emulated their prophet in every respect, from his manners to dress to diet, so it was no accident that great teachers became more prophetic as they manifested more courage, compassion, and humility for the sake of civilization. I once saw a photo in the *Guinness Book of World Records* of a man hauling a steam engine with his teeth. Men like Martin Luther King and the Shaykh reminded me of that guy: they bore down on truth and refused to let go, leaned into it and gave everything they had to move this great sluggish engine of humanity forward just a few inches before they gave out.

The first time I saw my husband put his forehead to the

254 | KRISTA BREMER

ground in prayer, through a crack in his bedroom door when he thought he was alone, I was as disturbed as if I'd caught him piercing a voodoo doll with a needle. What kind of God, I wondered, would want us in such a compromised position? But worship is Islam's fundamental practice; Muslims cultivate a direct relationship with God through their five daily prayers. The more I listened to the Shaykh, the more I wondered about those prayers. Five times a day seemed excessive—unless I counted the number of times each day I lost focus, compulsively checked messages, got too distracted by busyness and daydreams to remember the single most important thing. Then it seemed infinitely small.

I knew from my writing and running routines what rewards came over time from disciplined practice, so I decided to perform the Salat, or Muslim prayer, for one month—just to see what happened. I did not discuss my prayer experiment. Meditation was hip, but prayer put me in league with strutting televangelists, histrionic abortion-clinic protesters, homophobic politicians with lurid sexual secrets. And Muslim prayer was even worse.

I HAD ALWAYS had a hard time taking instruction from my husband, but thanks to Google, I didn't have to in this case. I found a website to guide me through the motions, with an audio file to teach me Arabic pronunciation. In my bedroom I moved awkwardly through the positions. With the help of a free download, I turned toward the Kaaba, Islam's holiest site, which Muslims everywhere face in prayer. I stood noble and tall, as God's representative on earth, then bowed at the waist, then folded all the way down to the ground like the lowliest of servants. My body strained to embody nobility and servitude, strength and powerlessness. That repeated up-and-down movement dislodged something deep inside. The weight of my forehead against the ground broke apart what I'd spent a lifetime trying to protect: my fragile individualism and brittle self-determination. With my face to the ground, an oppressive weight rolled off my shoulders: the burdensome arrogance and guilt that came from believing I was master of my life, the sole source of its brokenness and beauty. I began to weep for all I did not understand and could not control.

It was not easy to pray first thing in the morning, just before bed, and in stolen moments of privacy throughout the day. I only discussed my experience with one wise and luminous friend. Her serenity and strength did not come from taking yoga classes, listening to Eckhart Tolle CDs in her car, or attending Buddhist retreats in Big Sur. She paid dearly for her maturity a few years ago, when her husband was struck with leukemia and died a few months later, leaving her with a five-year-old son to raise.

The morning after her husband died, we sat together at her kitchen table drafting his obituary. Not long after the funeral she attacked her front yard, hacking away at crab grass and slamming the shovel's metal blade into hard North Carolina clay the color of rust. She built a garden, enclosed it in a high deer fence, planted vegetables and marigolds. When I visited her in summertime, she filled my cupped hands with brilliant yellow flowers whose petals appeared to have been dipped in blood.

"A strange thing has happened," I told her. "I've begun to pray—and it actually *helps* me." After two weeks, the change was subtle but undeniable. I was more patient and grateful. Anxiety was loosening its grip. Meditation emptied my mind, but prayer filled my heart.

My friend hugged me. "I'm so glad for you," she said, and her happiness lit up the room like sunlight.

"I just can't understand *why* it works," I went on. "Do I sound crazy? Is it a placebo effect? Am I deluding myself?"

She put her hands over her ears, groaned, and rolled her eyes.

"Please, stop! For God's sake, if it's working, don't overanalyze it!"

After I'd been listening to the Shaykh for over a year, I had the opportunity to attend one of his *khutbas,* or public sermons, while I was on a cross-country trip. A low-budget Internet video denigrating the prophet Muhammad had recently led to explosive protests in Egypt, Libya, Pakistan, and elsewhere. Meanwhile, four Americans, including the American ambassador to Libya, had been murdered during an attack on the American embassy in Benghazi. The Shaykh had been giving impassioned speeches against violence and fundamentalism. "I adopted this faith," he said at a Friday sermon in Northern

California, "and I am sick of defending ignorant, backward, re-actionary fools." At the same time, he challenged non-Muslim Americans to consider why this country refuses to tolerate the vilification of an ethnicity but allows the vilification of a faith. Did Americans realize that Jesus and the other prophets were as beloved to Muslims as was their prophet Muhammad? He had thrust himself into the middle of a volatile confrontation and was taking on both sides. He looked exhausted: smaller, more fragile in person.

After his sermon was over, I approached him to ask if I could take a photo. He smiled a tired smile, put his palm out like a gussied-up Indian at a roadside tourist attraction, and made a cynical joke: *Five dollars,* he said. I wanted to tell him I was no tourist and he was no prop; I was looking for far more than a souvenir. But in a sense he was right: I wanted to capture his soul in a photo, to steal some of his spirit to take home with me.

Beside my bed is a bookshelf that holds all the spiritual texts I've acquired over the years. Some nights, unable to sleep, I lie on my side and study the spines of those books: so many years of searching, so many different ways to describe the mystery at the heart of our lives. I propped the Shaykh's photo on the bookshelf. Later, as I thumbed through my closet looking for the right outfit, I glanced up and saw his face, and was re-minded that not just the dress but the body is a costume, that it will grow wrinkled and worn and finally be gone. I began to think about beautiful actions instead.

21 | *Celebration*

I once had a boyfriend in California who inherited sky blue eyes from his father, along with a taste for pricey liquor and a penchant for designer brands. He picked me up for dates in a convertible that had been a graduation present: a car like a toy, candy-apple red with gleaming chrome. He taught me how to order sushi, mix a strong martini, throw a party that lasted until the early hours of the morning. The year I moved in with him, small square envelopes began to appear in the mailbox of the studio that we shared: invitations with our names written in flowery script and that, when opened, scattered matching sheets of paper across the floor. All at once and without warning, our friends were starting to get married. Like the first summer heat that makes sweat pearl on skin, these wedding invitations were a sign that a new season was upon us—but we didn't realize that at the time. We saw these weddings as a chance to get dressed up, dance through the night, and enjoy free food and booze.

To each wedding we attended that summer, I wore a velvet floor-length dress with a plunging neckline that hugged my body like a second skin. My boyfriend had selected it for me at a store where carpet muffled our feet and a saleswoman hovered around us in a cloud of flowery perfume. He wore a black suit whose jacket draped across his broad back and pants that brushed his polished shoes as if they were made for him. On summer afternoons, we drove to beachside wedding ceremonies with the top down on his car. The air was soft as melting butter; a warm wind whipped at our faces. We arrived late and found ourselves a seat in the back row, where his hand crept up my velvety thigh while the minister's grave tones echoed off cavernous walls. The vows our friends repeated to one another sounded stiff and archaic. When I heard the words "For better or for worse," I leaned in close to my boyfriend, rolled my eyes, and whispered "That's the kicker," and we snickered. We agreed that weddings were fantastic fun and thought maybe we'd even get married one day if only we could eliminate those last three words—*or for worse*—which seemed tagged on to the ceremony like the warnings on medication commercials: potential side effects rattled off as quickly as possible, right after a warm voice has lulled you into believing that a particular pill is the solution to your hair loss or weight gain, your dull sex life or creeping despair.

AT ONE RECEPTION, the band played the first chords of Louis Armstrong's "What a Wonderful World" just as the fiery sun melted into a sea of glass, bathing the parquet dance floor in a warm glow. My boyfriend grabbed my hand and pulled me from my seat. He could not resist an empty dance floor: all that room to perform, all those flushed and hungry faces watching. His hand warmed the naked skin of my lower back as he pressed my body hard against him, and we began to twirl. The floor spun beneath us.

As we turned, I caught the eye of a white-haired man in polyester slacks, utterly still except for a thick, knobby finger circling the rim of his cocktail glass. He stared at us, transfixed, like we were an apparition: a ghost from his past or a storybook prince and princess come to life. The woman beside him watched us the same way, slack-jawed, her wrinkled face softening beneath thick layers of makeup. For the three minutes it took the band to play that song as the sun melted into the ocean, we were the focus of their naked longing and nostalgia; their admiring faces lit up the stage for our performance of love.

We made a spectacle of ourselves on that dance floor: our supple, hungry bodies, our shimmering ignorance, our cliche theatrics of romance. It was a moment of pure illusion. That young man who guided me so expertly across the dance floor did not know how to listen to me, challenge me, or comfort me when I cried. And despite the fact that I yielded so gracefully on the dance floor, I did not know how to apologize, to show gratitude, to accept him for who he was. Later that same night, he stumbled drunk from my bed and peed in my closet, all over the polyester work clothes I had just purchased for my new job. Years later, through a common friend, I would discover that while I was in the restroom that evening he had slipped into his pocket the phone number of the voluptuous hairdresser at our table. Our short-lived affair was like a binge, an ill-fated night on the town: we spent ourselves extravagantly, hopping from pleasure to pleasure, chasing a fading high even as a creeping void nipped at our heels. Right from the beginning we hurtled toward the end of us, our downfall accelerated by bad choices and deferred responsibilities. Our breakup was a blur of mounting exhaustion, sloppy rage, and a disturbing sense of disorientation: how had I gotten here and how would I ever find my way back home?

I knew nothing, absolutely *nothing*, about real love back then—but after being with Ismail for eight years, after creating a home and delivering two children, and trying and failing over and over again to juggle parenting and work and partnership, I did now. Real love was sitting outside on the front porch in the dark with him on a weeknight, after dinner had been eaten, dishes cleaned, books read, children showered and put to bed—and then chased down and tucked in again after they had stealthily crept from their rooms. We were too tired to talk, too tired to touch, too tired to do anything but sit side by side staring into the darkened street, taking long swigs of silence as if it were a stiff drink.

And then I tried to put into words what I couldn't say to

anyone else. I described the sadness that sometimes settled over me like a dense fog, obscuring the shape of my life. I told him there were days when I became utterly lost in our small house—when I wandered aimlessly from room to room, unable to find a path forward. For me, the most difficult part of parenting was not the sleepless nights, the financial responsibility, or even time's relentless forward momentum, like a moving sidewalk always carrying my children farther away from me. The hardest part was to remember *why* we did all this work to preserve our home and family. I wanted to show my children what a meaningful life looked like, to teach them that existence was about more than standing in straight lines at school and raising their hands before they spoke, keeping a home tidy and stocked with groceries, saving for college or retirement. But I was so exhausted and overwhelmed that I had forgotten the answer to the most important question.

"Sometimes I feel like I'm going crazy," I mumbled, staring straight ahead, not looking at Ismail, my eyes filling with tears.

He did not respond. After a moment, I felt his hand settle over mine, the calloused pad of his thumb stroking my skin.

"Then I will go crazy with you."

I glanced over at him, and when his eyes met mine, he shrugged. "Wherever you are, I want to be with you."

I sat there speechless, in my sweatpants and old tank top that sagged in the chest, looking out at the empty street. I did not lean in for a long kiss, or take him by the hand to lead him upstairs to our bedroom, or even tell him I loved him. He was wearing his flannel pajama pants with the red and pink polka dots—a gift from a previous Valentine's Day that had never suited him but he wore anyway. His face looked drawn. There was nothing else I wished for, nothing more precious or enduring than his words, which were swallowed up by the hungry darkness as soon as they were spoken.

IN OUR EARLY years as parents, after we had gone to the justice of the peace and recited the Fatiha before our Muslim friends, I had dismissed the idea of a wedding. But as the years passed, I began to feel it was important for family and friends to witness our vows—and after everything we had been through, I could think of no better reason for a party than to celebrate the endurance of our love and commitment. Eight years after we met, we finally had a wedding celebration at a farm in the North Carolina countryside, on a late-spring day when the heat was beginning to press in. Our children were three and eight years old. We hand-lettered invitations for our friends: *Aliya Rose and Khalil Zade invite you to celebrate the marriage of their parents.* We'd lived together so many years in this small town; I imagined friends' eyes widening in surprise when they opened the mail. "Honey, you won't *believe* whose wedding we were invited to today!" they might say over dinner that night. Was it too late for this? Would our friends think a celebration indulgent? Would they assume we hadn't been married before? It didn't matter. Something in me had shifted, and now the public ritual seemed important. We needed to stand before our community and affirm our commitment to each other and to this family.

The day of our wedding, Ismail and I went on an early-morning run down the same trails we had explored when we first met. The air was thick and fragrant with rain. We noticed a box turtle in our path—then another, then another, stopped smack in the middle of narrow trail. We knelt to admire the mottled yellow and brown shells slick with moisture. Later, I took a drive out into the country and down a gravel road to a flower farm, where a woman with long gray braids and a girlish smile packed dewy, tangled wildflowers into plastic buckets. I loaded them into my hatchback and even balanced some on my lap, so that I peered through flowers as I drove. Petals pressed against each window.

One of Ismail's oldest friends was a reclusive piano repairman who drove his battered red truck all over the countryside, tuning and fixing pianos in church basements and well-appointed living rooms. Over six feet tall with thick glasses, bushy eyebrows, and a long gray ponytail, Carlos spoke rarely and only in staccato bursts. When something struck him as funny, he snorted and blushed like a gangly adolescent. Only when he was seated at a piano, with his back to the world, did he seem completely at ease.

For our wedding he insisted on hauling a grand piano on

a flatbed trailer to the pine tree in the middle of the meadow where we planned to exchange our vows. "Seems like a heck of a lot of work for so little return," said my neighbor skeptically, as he stood in the shade the day of our wedding, watching the eight-hundred-pound piano being hauled slowly over potholes and through tall grass. But Carlos could not be dissuaded. He was not one to stand in front of our guests to deliver a toast; nor would he offer us a prettily wrapped present. His incomparable gift was to lean over his piano as we made our way arm in arm across the meadow that afternoon. As we approached, he cocked his head and seemed to listen for a message in the whispering breeze. Then he began to play. His fingers fluttered like butterflies over the notes; his music swooped and rose like a springtime cardinal.

It was a wanton, glorious act: a herculean effort for a fleeting moment of perfection. In the glow of a late-afternoon sun, Ismail and I walked hand in hand across that green meadow and into a pool of friends gathered in the shade of the pine tree. Their love washed over us like a gentle wave. We stood before a tree trunk my friend had garlanded with wildflowers. Our curly-haired son slept in my mother's lap in the front row; our dark-haired, long-limbed daughter walked a few feet ahead of us scattering petals along the path. A Muslim friend waited beneath the tree to lead the ceremony, the wings of his white robe whipping in the breeze. An elderly neighbor who sold flowers at the farmers' market and led the choir at the Baptist church sang us a gospel song a cappella. Our friend Jamal stood beneath the tree and recited a Rumi poem like a royal bard, turning his face toward the sun and sweeping his arms toward the sky:

Love comes like a knife.
Not some shy question,
And not with fears for its reputation.

I say these things disinterestedly—
Accept them in kind . . .

Love is a Madman!
Working his wild schemes, running
Through the mountains, drinking poison,
And now, quietly choosing annihilation.

My chest ached with the sweet pain of an overfull heart. When it was my turn to speak, a powerful and unexpected shyness arose in me. In a wavering voice, I thanked Ismail for showing me that love means surrender—and for giving me the incomparable freedom of being known and accepted as I was. I promised he would always have a home in my heart. When it was his turn, he thanked me for inspiring and challenging him, and he promised to keep growing and dreaming with me for the rest of his life. Our union felt as incongruous and un-expected as the shimmering black piano resting briefly in the shade of the tree—and it, too, required arduous work for fleeting moments of beauty and communion.

After the ceremony we moved to the barn, where our friends had covered two long banquet tables with homemade dishes from their native countries: empanadas and baklava, kibbeh and Congolese stew. Our friend and his son played bluegrass as our guests ate. When people began making toasts, Aliya raised her hand, and someone lifted her up onto a chair so she could face the crowd. She took the microphone in her hands. "I feel very lucky to be at my parents' wedding," she said. "Most kids don't get to do that." A ripple of laughter rolled through the room. I laughed as well, but my chuckle was nearly a sob. Her words were a benediction; like the key I had been searching for ever since I met Ismail, they threw open the door to gratitude for every turn my life had taken. Nothing about my life resembled the future I had once imagined—and for years I had grappled with resentment or regret because this path had never been easy. Now I saw that every single struggle had brought its own gifts; every unexpected turn had brought me to this moment.

Wendell Berry writes that guests at a wedding witness a death that shadows new life: two individuals die into their marital union the way a soul dies into God. The day after my wedding, when I returned to the abandoned barn to begin cleaning, signs of decay were everywhere. Brittle flowers turned inward under the harsh midday sun. Ismail and I went from table to table yanking them from vases of cloudy water and dropping them into piles on the ground. The long banquet table, yesterday covered in an unparalleled feast of offerings from a hundred friends, was covered now in crumbs and congealed spills that drew flies. Yesterday I had peeled this wedding dress from its plastic covering and slipped it over my scrubbed body, its pressed white layers hugging my scented skin. Today it had a blueberry smear across the skirt where a toddler had reached for me with a sticky hand, and a catch in the fabric where it caught the splintery edge of a wooden table. Its grimy hem skimmed over the gravel parking lot as I hauled it over my shoulder to my car. Today there were bottles to recycle, sheets to wash, payments to be made, children to be retrieved from the baby-sitter. The late-spring air prickled my skin like hot breath as we cleaned up the remains of our celebration. Today the heat was rising. Ours would always be a sticky marriage.

22 | *Home*

Two hours before her first rock concert, Aliya was on the computer using the Internet to translate her fan letter to her favorite band, Tinariwen, into French. Formed more than thirty years ago in a Libyan refugee camp, Tinariwen produces a hypnotic blend of West African blues, reggae, and rock, all melted together as if they have been left out in the desert sun. The band members are Tuareg, nomads who have lived in the Sahara for millennia. After some of them rebelled against the Malian government in the early sixties, thousands of Tuaregs fled into Libya and Algeria, and an entire generation was raised in refugee camps, cut off from their traditional way of life. Ibrahim Ag Alhabib, the founder of Tinariwen, was one of them. In the late seventies Western rock music reached the camps, and Ibrahim heard Jimi Hendrix, Led Zeppelin, and Bob Marley. As a boy he built his own guitar from a stick, a tin can, and a bicycle brake wire.

Aliya had been listening to Tinariwen for as long as she

could remember. Her father relished their ballads about oppression and exile. Their love songs to Africa were like meandering paths that led Ismail back to the continent he left behind when he fled Muammar Gaddafi's dictatorial rule. On his commute to and from his corporate job, Ismail turned their music up so loud that his car windows vibrated. On nights when we got tangled in a web of accusations and misunderstandings—when he looked at me and saw a selfish, materialistic American, and I looked at him and saw an overbearing, irrational African, and we each felt impossibly far from home—he retreated to the living room, cradled his head in his hands, and listened to this music as if it were counsel from a trusted friend. On those rare weekend mornings when he surprised us with a traditional Libyan breakfast, we listened to Tinariwen as we rolled pasty white dough between our fingers and dipped it into sticky date syrup as thick and black as tar.

Aliya loved her father more than any other man in the world. So it seemed impossible for her not to love Tinariwen. She had been looking forward to this concert—held at a local nightclub that opens past her bedtime—for months.

"YOU'RE TAKING HER to a *rock concert*? With a bunch of *drunks*?"

Our friend Jamal's voice rose in exaggerated alarm when he found out. It was early evening, and we were seated cross-legged on our carpet, drinking tea with him and his wife,

Maryam. Aliya had just told him how excited she was about the upcoming show, and now he was looking at Ismail and me, smiling and shaking his head and making Aliya giggle nervously.

Formerly a day trader named Sam who was raised Jewish, Jamal was now a devout Muslim who avoided most music and movies because he said they stole his focus away from God. He displayed only Islamic art in his home, avoided cookies that contained vanilla (it had a trace of alcohol in it), and refused silverware when he joined us for dinner, instead lifting curry and rice to his mouth with his fingers just as the prophet Muhammad did fourteen hundred years ago. Over the course of our friendship I had come to see how his strict practices polished his heart to a high shine. Thoughtful and soft-spoken, he was one of the most sincere people I knew. He was teasing us about the concert, but I felt the sharp sting of judgment in his words: I would be taking my daughter on a field trip to Gomorrah, a forsaken space where sweaty people guzzled beer and pressed together in the dark, getting as close as they could to an explosion of sound that made them briefly forget the world.

Before we sat down to tea and almonds, Jamal and Ismail stood side by side in the fading light of our living room, hands crossed over their stomachs, and faced Mecca to perform the Maghrib prayer. But before Ismail began to recite, Jamal asked abruptly, "Do you mind if I check the direction of Mecca?" He pulled his phone from his pocket, tapped its screen, and studied it like a man lost in the wilderness. The app pointed straight as an arrow toward the Holy Land from anywhere on the globe. Jamal told Ismail they should reposition themselves a few degrees to the left.

"Of course," Ismail said, a smile tugging at his lips. He later told me that he would turn around and pray backward if Jamal asked him to: "As far as I'm concerned, we face Allah in any direction we turn."

I envied Jamal's absolute clarity about his beliefs, his precise faith like a GPS showing him where he stood at all times. I didn't have such clear convictions. Instead I clung to my splintered identity as if it were flotsam on a stormy sea. For years Ismail and I had been raising our children in the rocky terrain between my secular Western culture and his Muslim North African one, on the ever-shifting sands between ambition and modesty, desire and humility, self-determination and surrender to God. I was a part-time Buddhist who overlooked the prohibition against alcohol as if it were a bill I couldn't afford to pay. I cared about environmental issues—but apparently not as much as I cared about a cappuccino in a to-go cup on a Monday morning or a house cool enough in summer to make my skin prickle and warm enough in winter that I could walk around barefoot. I was a feminist who expected her husband to make more money than she did, a mother who dreamed of taking her annual vacations alone.

When I was around Jamal, I began to question the wisdom of raising my children in this disputed territory. Maybe our daughter and son needed solid ground beneath their feet as much as they did a roof over their head. Maybe they needed one of us to leave behind his or her old habits so they could finally settle into a single coherent worldview. But without his Islam or his African ways, Ismail would be a stranger to me—and though I loved him, I wasn't sure I loved him enough to give up rock music, chocolate-chip cookies, or shorts in summertime.

THERE WAS ANOTHER reason Aliya was buzzing with excitement about this concert: her father had promised that she would get to spend time backstage with Tinariwen. I didn't understand how he could make this promise, since he had no connection to any of the band members. He appeared never to have considered the possibility that he wouldn't be able to fulfill it. Instead he'd been asking Aliya what she planned to discuss with her idols, leading her to believe that they would welcome her like a member of their tribe. With such unrealistic expectations, how could she not end up disappointed?

When she was younger, Aliya used to take pride in her father's Libyan upbringing, bragging to her friends that he was raised in a mud hut and watching in awe as he turned rusty bottle caps and old string into spinning toys, sticks and deer pellets into whirling helicopters. But lately she'd been less amused by his African ways. They'd been going head-to-head over how many pairs of shoes a sixth-grader needs (*One*, he said), whether she should have a cell phone (*Are you kidding me?*), how she should respond to him when he called her (*Yes, Baba*), and how much she should get paid for watching her little brother (*When I was your age, I took care of five siblings for no money at all*). I was worried that tonight he would finally fall from the pedestal on which he had been teetering ever since she entered middle school.

An hour before the show, Aliya was standing before her open closet, studying her wardrobe, trying to choose just the right outfit in which to meet her favorite band. Perhaps one of her new head scarves: the pink one with shimmering gold thread that caught the light, or the gauzy yellow one from Morocco that made her face look like it was swaddled in sun. On our back porch one afternoon last summer, a Muslim friend of ours showed her how to sweep her hair beneath a scarf, pull the fabric tight and low across her forehead, and tie a neat knot at the base of her neck. When she was done, Aliya turned to me and scanned my face as if it were a mirror. She looked like a North African queen, eyes like dark chocolate nickels, lips so full and perfect that the moment I first saw them, the day she was born, I knew her middle name would be Rose.

Now she was contemplating her head scarves, neatly folded in her closet beside her hoodies and T-shirts, trying to decide which one to wear tonight. Each time she walked out the door with her head covered, the grown-up world around her divided in two. Some of our friends showered her with compliments, whereas others cast nervous glances in her direction and avoided mentioning it. She was either a beloved member of the Muslim tribe or part of a herd, broken of her American independence and corralled into Islam. But Aliya was unfazed. She understood what she was wearing: a soft, colorful cloth that made her feel beautiful; a symbol of the modesty she carried in her heart, whether her head was covered or not; a sign of the faith she had been learning from her father's example since the day she was born, just as she had learned how to make date cookies scented with rose water.

Aliya came downstairs a few minutes later wearing jeans, a FREE LIBYA T-shirt, and a head scarf her aunt gave her. This year she had shed the last of her baby fat and grown skinny and moody and long. Tonight she looked part Muslim revolutionary, part American preteen—which, of course, is exactly what she was: a girl balancing, sometimes gracefully, sometimes awkwardly, between her father's world and mine.

WE PULLED INTO a strip-mall parking lot, empty except for the band's tour bus, which was backed into a corner and cordoned off with yellow tape, each glowing window blocked by a curtain. In our house Tinariwen may have been the biggest band of the twenty-first century, but in our southern college town it was a little-known African group playing world music on a Sunday night at a club that shared its lot with a pizza place and a convenience store.

Before I had even removed my key from the ignition, Ismail and Aliya jumped from the car. They crossed the lot and began talking to two men in black leather jackets who were smoking outside the bus—part of the road crew. Ismail smiled and shook their hands while Aliya hung back, clutching her carefully folded fan letter. Despite Ismail's friendly greeting, the leather-jacketed men didn't let them past the tape. One craned his neck to get a look at this four-and-a-half-foot-tall girl in the FREE LIBYA shirt and head scarf.

I waited by the entrance to the club, where a poster of the band was taped to a darkened window littered with the tattered edges of last week's fliers. In the picture the musicians stood in a desert beside a parched tree whose spindly branches reached toward them like black claws. The wind pressed their colorful ankle-length robes against their bodies, and layers of cloth covered most of each band member's face. A pure blue sky floated above, and the Sahara beneath their feet was like a brilliant white carpet. The North Africa of this poster was a barren but beautiful place where people bloomed from nothing and grew like cacti in the harsh desert sun. It was as much a fairy tale to me as the North Africa of Ismail's childhood, where mothers nursed one another's children and people brought livestock into their homes to keep them warm on cold desert nights. These stories had nothing to do with the Africa

I saw in the news: a land of tyranny, civil war, and widespread health epidemics. The Libya I discovered when I visited there in 2005 bore little resemblance to the tragic yet idyllic Africa of my imagination.

As the parking lot began to fill up, the men in leather jackets stubbed their cigarettes out on the oil-stained asphalt and disappeared through the bus's narrow door. People were milling around outside the club. A man in a Grateful Dead T-shirt ran a hand through his stringy gray hair. A woman swished past in a floral skirt. Traffic hummed relentlessly in the background, car exhaust thickening the cool night air. Aliya was still holding her fan letter, trying to determine her next move. Time was running out; the opening band would start to play in fifteen minutes.

"Give me the letter," Ismail said, holding out his hand. Aliya yanked the ragged piece of notebook paper out of his reach, eyeing him with suspicion.

"What are you going to do with it?"

"I'm going to get on the bus and give it to the band," he said with such calm, clear conviction that it almost made trespassing sound like a rational thing to do.

A familiar apprehension arose in me. Ismail had a way of plowing through personal boundaries as if he didn't even see them, then reacting with genuine surprise when I pointed out his faux pas. Not realizing that grown-ups in the United States usually kept a polite distance from children who weren't theirs, Ismail reached out for neighborhood kids, mussing their hair or reprimanding them as if they were his own, never noticing the nervous looks of their parents. At dinner parties, Ismail would casually ask the host how much he paid for his house or bemoan U.S. intervention in the Middle East. The other guests would suddenly notice their empty glasses and excuse themselves.

Years ago, at a stuffy restaurant where couples sat at small round tables and whispered over flickering candles, I told Ismail I was pregnant with our second child. His eyes filled with tears, and he swept his arms wide as if to embrace the entire room. "Hey, everyone—we're going to have a baby!" he boomed, as if these strangers were part of his extended family, as if his joy were like champagne that he could pour and share with everyone present. An awkward silence followed as people looked embarrassed on our behalf.

Now I was seriously considering whether his bursting onto the bus would qualify as breaking and entering. Aliya was biting her lower lip and looking back and forth between us. She could probably have used some guidance, but I was at a loss. Respecting personal boundaries was like a religion for me. I wasn't one to show up unannounced or to barge through closed doors, and I had a hard enough time asking friends for favors, let alone strangers.

It was a small comfort for me to discover while in Libya that Ismail was not unique; many Libyans had this endearing, maddening blindness to personal space. Perhaps the reason I was so guarded is that I never lived among extended family. I knew relatives mostly through the presents that arrived in the mail and the thank-you cards I sent in return. Though it was true that by maintaining my polite distance I had successfully avoided imposing myself on others, it was also true that my husband had many more friends he could call in the middle of the night.

Looking exasperated with both of us, Aliya took our hands and pulled us toward the open doors of the club. Inside, we found a spot at the edge of the stage, and the opening band began to play. A few minutes later, when I turned to ask Ismail and Aliya if they liked the music, they were gone.

THE OTHER DAY, when I was walking home from the grocery store with Aliya, she said out of the blue, "Sometimes I feel bad for Dad, because people here don't understand him very well." She wasn't talking about his accent but about the way he is perceived: the way her friends scrunched up their noses at his spicy food or retreated from the sound of his loud voice, the way her teachers spoke patronizingly to him, the way some of our friends squirmed when his eyes filled with tears in a culture that had little room for crying men. She understood that to be an immigrant was to live in a country of misunderstandings, to be obscured by stereotypes and prejudice.

Then Aliya cocked her head at me, considering me thoughtfully for a moment. "People misunderstand you too, Mom, because you sort of hover in between places, so they don't know what to make of you."

It was true. Ismail was not the only immigrant in our family. To make this life with him, I've had to leave behind much of my upbringing, putting an ocean of differences between myself and loved ones. Ismail would never play golf or watch sports on television with the men in my family, and they would never see the world from the point of view of the colonized, the stateless, and the oppressed. A gulf divides them, forcing me to commute long distances between their realities. Each December, when Ismail needed to be reminded how to celebrate Christmas, I felt homesick for the country I had left behind, where holiday rituals never had to be taught. Between the two of us we now had twice as many holidays to celebrate, one of us always the determined apprentice to the other.

Even some of my old friends regarded Ismail with skepticism. I've had to accept their general discomfort around him and their assumption, in spite of overwhelming evidence to the contrary, that he was a controlling Muslim husband. At a party one night a Cat Stevens song came on the radio, and an old friend grabbed my arm. "Oh, I love Cat Stevens!" she said.

"So do I."

"I couldn't believe it when he went off the deep end into

that whole 'Yusuf Islam' thing. I was like, 'Dude, what happened to the peace train?'" She rolled her eyes as she tilted her glass to her lips.

I wanted to say, *Islam is his peace train. He got on it and rode away, and he's been on it ever since.* But she probably wouldn't have heard me; she was standing on a distant shore where Islam and peace were categorical opposites, a place where I once lived but to which I could never return. Sometimes I still missed its soothing homogeneity, its bright illusions of superiority and invincibility.

And yet I still looked like I belonged in that place, whereas my husband and daughter looked like they belonged to each other, with their big dark eyes and cafe-au-lait skin. Everywhere I went, it seemed, couples were paired up like two of a kind on Noah's ark: toned men and women jogging down the street in matching spandex; ruddy-faced couples in identical team colors hauling their cooler to a football game; Muslim couples in flowing garments touching their foreheads to the ground in prayer. Sometimes I wondered if Noah would even let Ismail and me on the boat, or if he'd stop us as we walked up the gangplank, pointing out as gently as he could that we were not, in fact, a matching pair.

So I had often felt alone — just as I did right now, standing in this crowded club in the dark.

After a forty-five-minute set the opening band bowed and

left the stage, the lights came up, and there were the leather-jacketed men onstage, unrolling cables, adjusting mikes, and tuning instruments for the band. A murmur of anticipation coursed through the room. Just before the members of Tinariwen made their appearance, Aliya's hand slipped into mine. Her eyes were blazing.

"Guess where I've been, Mom: hanging out on the bus with the band!"

Behind her Ismail beamed at me, one eyebrow raised as if to say, *Who's doubting me now?*

Later he would tell me what happened. He and Aliya wandered back outside, where they found the drummer standing beside the bus, smoking a cigarette. *"As-salaamu alaykum,"* Ismail said, his hand pressed over his heart. *Peace be with you.* The man looked up, startled, as if recognizing the voice of an old friend. When Ismail said he was from Libya, the drummer held the door of the bus open and urged them to come inside.

They climbed the narrow steps to find the rest of the band seated at a small table in the back. Ismail greeted them in Arabic, his hand over his heart, and told them how much he and his daughter loved their music, and about Aliya's letter. She held out the folded piece of notebook paper, damp and creased from her sweaty fingers, like a crumpled white flag. Ibrahim, whose charcoal Afro hung like a storm cloud over his weathered face, who saw his father executed when he was just four years old, stood up to retrieve it. He bowed his head and put his hand over his heart in gratitude. Abdallah, one of the guitarists, called for the rest of the band to listen as he read her letter aloud:

I am eleven years old and I have been listening to your music for my whole life. I want to tell you how much I love it; the sound of your music is unique and wonderful. I am so excited I can barely write this letter because I know I will be seeing you tonight. My dad is from Libya. You are my heroes. I hope that one day I will have a band like yours.

Abdallah knelt down, took Aliya's hand in his, and spoke to her in Arabic.

"We are honored to receive this letter from you," he said. "This is the beginning of a long friendship between you and Tinariwen."

Then they invited her and Ismail to join them around the small table, and the drummer poured them strong, sweet green tea in glass cups like the ones that warmed my palm every day I spent in Libya. For nearly an hour Aliya sat sandwiched between her father and Ibrahim, cradling a steaming cup while the men chatted and joked in Arabic. When a member of the sound crew popped his head onto the bus to announce that it was ten minutes until showtime, Ibrahim told Aliya that if she grew tired during the show, she was welcome to return to the bus to rest, and that our entire family could come back for more tea after the show was over. They left her a folded blanket and showed her where to lie down.

Ismail did, in fact, have powerful connections to the band, connections called "Africa" and "exile." He understood what I'd failed to grasp: that when he led Aliya up the narrow stairs of the tour bus, he was leading her back to the deserts of North Africa, where those who have been driven from their homes recognized the longing in one another's eyes, where unexpected guests were treated like nobility and children like family.

Ismail had a habit of beckoning to our son and daughter when they were beyond his reach, saying, "Give us a kiss." Before our children disappeared upstairs to bed or after they had said something funny or sad or when the light hit their faces just so and he was pierced by their innocence, he reached out to them from where he sat alone: *Give us a kiss.*

I sometimes wanted to correct his use of the plural pronoun, but I held my tongue because I knew he didn't learn to speak English until well into adulthood, and I found his unconventional grammar endearing. I had, however, joked with Aliya about her father's expression.

Aliya used to kiss us both every night before bed, but lately she just drifted up to her room when we were unaware, and it wasn't until I was lying in bed myself that I realized I hadn't kissed her all day. The other night she was halfway up the stairs when Ismail called after her, "Give us a kiss," and she turned slowly and made her way back down, feigning reluctance but smiling anyway. First she kissed his stubbly cheek, then the air beside him, as if an invisible person were sitting there. She looked at me and giggled at our private joke. Ismail smiled quizzically at us.

"What's funny? Did I say something incorrectly?"

"It's just that it makes no sense to say 'us' when you are sitting there alone," I explained. "When you say it that way, it sounds like you are referring to the imaginary friend by your side."

He grew quiet, contemplating this.

"But it's a direct translation of what we say to children in Libya. It wouldn't be right to say 'Give me a kiss,' excluding all the other adults in the room."

I recalled how, when I was in Libya, my mother-in-law's house was crowded day and night with hordes of relatives eager to see Ismail's American wife and child. Each time we entered the home, my coat was slipped from my shoulders, and five-year-old Aliya was swept from my arms and passed around the room like candy for everyone to taste. When she was finally returned to me, her plump cheeks were rosy from being pressed to so many lips, squeezed by so many hands. It wasn't just relatives but also shopkeepers in the market, waiters in restaurants. Once, an elderly Iraqi refugee we met on the street cradled Aliya's smooth cheeks between leathery hands and spoke to her in a steady stream of Arabic, ignoring me altogether, as if they shared a secret.

NOW IBRAHIM, THE lead singer, walked onstage, his silken tunic covering everything but his cowboy boots and the hems of his gold-threaded pants. Deep lines traversed his face like well-traveled paths. He scanned the cheering crowd with the somber love of a father watching his children sleep. Then he leaned into the microphone and spoke.

"The best language in the world," he said in French, "is music. When I try to speak any of the others, it's a catastrophe."

His fingers plucked the strings of his guitar as if they had a life of their own, and he began to sing, his gravelly voice gaining momentum like a rusty engine turning over and then humming on an open road. As he sang *"Subhan Allah"* ("Glory be to God"), the drummer kept pace, becoming a frenzy of motion, his hands slapping and pounding and sliding across animal skin. At the foot of the stage, a man whose beefy shoulders were black with tattoos closed his eyes and nodded in emphatic agreement with the sound. Aliya's skinny body bent toward the music like a sapling toward the sun. She crossed her arms over her chest, as if holding herself back from falling into the ocean of rhythm. Then her hands found each another and she began to clap.

Onstage a gray-haired dancer swayed his hips, his arms twisting and gliding through the air. The light in his eyes was brilliant. When he raised his hands to clap, I couldn't help but do the same; when he moved to the music, so did I. His joy fanned out around him like wildfire, setting ablaze in me a fierce longing, a hunger far too voracious to be satisfied by food, drink, or touch.

I believed that Allah could be found in the precision of Islam's rituals and the punctuality of its five daily prayers. But Allah was here, too, in this darkened club—in the red electric guitar swishing against a silken djellaba, in the brown fingers that strummed the chords. Allah was in the frenzied palms of the drummer slapping against a gourd as smooth and hard as stone. Allah was in the joyous old African man with the dancing feet of a child, gently coaxing us to peel off these stifling layers of craving, anxiety, and self-doubt and show our naked selves. Allah was the music, and we were swimming in it; it was washing us clean, its rhythms beating in time with our hearts. The air in the crowded room smelled of sweat. The bottle in my hand was growing warm. We didn't have much time—the song was already almost over, and soon we would all return to where we came from—but right now the old man was beckoning, inviting each of us to step inside the music, if only for a moment, and make ourselves at home.

ACKNOWLEDGMENTS

This book was made possible by many acts of kindness. I would like to thank the Rona Jaffe Foundation, the North Carolina Arts Council, the Bread Loaf Writers' Conference, and the Vermont Studio Center for supporting my work. Thanks to Michelle Cacho-Negrete for encouragement and inspiration from the very beginning, and to Greg Martin for insightful feedback on an early draft. Thanks to Jin Auh at the Wylie Agency for her acumen and heart—and to Craig Popelars, Kathy Pories, Ina Stern, Anne Winslow, Kelly Bowen, and the rest of the talented staff at Algonquin, with whom I am honored to work and in whose bright company I always want to linger. Thanks to my colleagues at *The Sun* magazine—my surrogate family in the south—and especially to Sy Safransky, incomparable mentor and friend. Abiding gratitude to Hamza Yusuf Hanson. Thanks to my Libyan family, who showed me the beauty of faith and the meaning of welcome; and to my parents, John and Suzanne Bremer, for instilling in me an open heart and an adventurous spirit, without which this journey would not be possible. Thanks to my children, Aliya Rose and Khalil Zade, who teach me daily about presence and joy; and to Ismail Suayah, muse and midwife to every page. In your tender heart I found my home.

A Tender Struggle

Questions for Discussion

Questions for Discussion

1. How does the author's definition of *jihad* (page 95) differ from its common usage in the media—and what does jihad have to do with her love story?

2. How does the author's understanding of the hijab (head covering) change when she is in Libya? What benefits and drawbacks does she discover in modest Muslim clothing—and what benefits and drawbacks does she identify from the physical exposure she experienced growing up in Southern California?

3. When she first arrives in Libya, the author pities her female Muslim relatives—but she is she surprised to discover that they pity her as well. Which aspects of her Western life might they pity, and how does her time in Libya make her rethink notions of freedom and oppression?

4. How does the author's understanding of feminism and surrender change over the course of the book? Is surrender at odds with feminism? Is surrender synonymous with defeat?

5. In what ways does the author's marriage change her opinions about diversity and tolerance?

6. The author encounters a dying grandmother during a family gathering in Libya. How does this woman's experience differ from aging and dying in the United States? What benefits and drawbacks can you identify in her experience?

7. What are specific examples of Islamophobia in the book? What does the author's experience convey about intolerance and the perception of otherness in the West?

8. In many ways, this book is about the search for home. What does the author convey about home in the final chapter—and do you agree with her definition?

9. Would you call this a strong marriage? Why or why not?

10. In what ways does the author's husband affirm or contradict common stereotypes about Muslim men?

11. Do you agree or disagree with the author's assertion that every relationship is bicultural? Which aspects of the author's struggle are particular to her marriage, and which aspects are universal?

BRIANA BROUGH

Krista Bremer is the associate publisher of *The Sun* and the recipient of the Rona Jaffe Foundation award. Her essay on which this book is based, "My Accidental Jihad," received a Pushcart Prize. Her essays have been published in *O: The Oprah Magazine*, *More* magazine, and *The Sun*, and have been translated and reprinted all over the world. She's been featured on NPR and in the PBS series *Arab American Stories*. She lives in North Carolina with her husband and her two children. Find her at www.kristabremer.com.